EDITED BY **MICHAEL ROBOTHAM**

IF I TELL YOU...
I'LL HAVE TO
KILL YOU

AUSTRALIA'S LEADING CRIME WRITERS
REVEAL THEIR SECRETS

ALLEN&UNWIN
SYDNEY · MELBOURNE · AUCKLAND · LONDON

First published in 2013

Allen & Unwin
Sydney, Melbourne, Auckland, London

83 Alexander Street
Crows Nest NSW 2065
Australia
Phone: (61 2) 8425 0100
Email: info@allenandunwin.com
Web: www.allenandunwin.com

Cataloguing-in-Publication details are available
from the National Library of Australia
www.trove.nla.gov.au

ISBN 978 1 74331 348 0

Internal text design by Squirt Creative
Set in 11.5/16 pt Bembo by Midland Typesetters, Australia
Printed in Australia by McPherson's Printing Group

10 9 8 7 6 5 4 3 2 1

MIX
Paper from
responsible sources
FSC® C001695

The paper in this book is FSC® certified.
FSC® promotes environmentally responsible,
socially beneficial and economically viable
management of the world's forests.

CONTENTS

INTRODUCTION: YOU'VE BEEN WARNED

by Michael Robotham

So you want to know where the bodies are buried. Don't say you weren't warned. When you delve into the minds of crime writers you are opening up a stinky stew of psychoses, superstitions, half-finished stories and unplanned homicides.

People often imagine that crime writers would be good at getting away with murder, but I can't even steal a kiss. Or to quote Woody Allen, I'm the sort of guy who, if I played baseball, would steal second base, feel guilty and go back. That's not to say I don't have murderous thoughts. I do . . . All the time. I contemplated killing the author of *Eat Pray Love* and then I wanted to kill the person who made it into a movie.

This may seem extreme but I'm not alone. In separate studies, two American psychologists, Douglas Kenrick and David Buss, asked people if they had ever fantasised about killing someone. The demographic they chose had exceptionally low rates of violence, yet between seventy and ninety per cent of men and between fifty and eighty per cent of women admitted to having at least one homicidal fantasy in the preceding year.

So there's no point in lying. I know you've day-dreamed about slipping rat poison into the boss's coffee or pushing your mother-in-law under a bus. And don't get me started on the neighbour who mows his lawn at 6.30 a.m. every Sunday. You're dead pal! Just try it next week!

Despite our day jobs, we crime writers are a collegiate, happy-go-lucky bunch. We put our dark thoughts on the page rather than bottling them up inside. You'll appreciate this as you read through these essays, which are written with enormous generosity, insight and humour. From the opening pages when Shane Maloney admits to having killed seventeen people, you will find bodies at every turn, as well as suspects, perpetrators and heroes.

This isn't a book about perfect crimes. It is about imperfect ones. A perfect murder, by its very definition, is one committed by a complete stranger who has never met the victim, has no criminal record, steals nothing and tells no one. For a crime to be truly perfect it can never be detected, which doesn't leave a lot of room for a writer. We need our murders to be imperfect, with grander or baser motives.

Our protagonists are a mixed bunch, ranging from whisky-soaked private eyes to ex-strippers, political fixers, wealthy aristocrats, former models, trembling psychologists, paramedics, pathologists, Aboriginal community police officers, detective inspectors, bikies and amateur sleuths. This is testament to the broad scope of crime writing in Australia, as the gender, jurisdictions and locations constantly change, but the fundamental elements remain: the crime, the investigation, the resolution and the ticking of the clock. It may not be tidy, it may not be nice, it may be bloody miserable, but justice is normally done.

Whether you're a fan of crime fiction or true crime, or a would-be crime writer yourself, you'll find laughter, understanding, insight, ideas, advice and hopefully some inspiration in this collection of essays. I was fascinated to read how other writers approach their craft. Some are plotters and some are 'pantsers' (writing by the seat of their pants). Some are pioneers and some are settlers. Some write what they know and others go to extraordinary lengths for the sake of their research, including being strangled to the point of unconsciousness.

After reading these essays I knew these writers better because I learned about the highs and lows, as well as the nuts and bolts of their working lives. Some stumbled into crime writing by accident, while others were raised on the genre being suckled on Chandler, Conan Doyle and Christie. For most of us it began as a passionate hobby and grew into something more. Peter Corris has been writing virtually every day for over thirty years and regards it as something akin to breathing—'stop it and I'd die'.

Those of us who read crime fiction and true crime stories appreciate these efforts because we take pleasure in the details and we love seeing the patterns behind the details. Fierce mental energy is needed to expose the lies and resolve the contradictions, to pull off the false beards, to interrogate witnesses and interpret the evidence. We also know that most modern crime stories are more than just mysteries. They are laden with insights about people, environments, politics, the law and much more. One week we can be on the mean streets of Chicago with Sara Paretsky or in Martha's Vineyard with Philip Craig or in Venice with Donna Leon and Sweden with Henning Mankell.

Crime stories allow us to escape from our daily lives and provide us with the reassurance that we can cope with our daily lives. They show us the best and worst of human nature and allow us to question how we would react in similar circumstances. Author Sue Grafton summed it up when she said: 'A crime story is more than a novel, more than a compelling account of people whose fate engages us. The mystery is a means by which we can explore, vicariously, the perplexing questions of crime, guilt and innocence, violence and justice.'

So consider yourself warned before you begin digging

up the bodies. Our secrets are now yours. And remember what Stephen King said when asked why he wrote about such gruesome subjects. 'Why do you assume that I have a choice?'

Michael Robotham

All royalties from this book go towards the Australian Crime Writers Association, which runs the annual Ned Kelly Awards and was established to promote crime writing and reading in Australia. If you'd like to learn more about the ACWA and see the benefits of membership go to our website: www.auscrimewriters.com

KEEP THE BODIES COMING

by Shane Maloney

So far I've killed around seventeen people. It's hard to be completely sure without digging them up and counting them all, but I've been at it for a while now and it has to be somewhere in the high teens, minimum. Among others, I've dispatched a leading-hand storeman, a promising young athlete, a talented painter, a shifty property developer, an abalone poacher, the owner of a trattoria in Moonee Ponds, a senior union official, a refrigeration mechanic, a public policy analyst, a gym jockey and both sons of a trucking magnate. I've frozen, drowned, bludgeoned, shot, speared, squashed, run down and incinerated them. And I still haven't finished. Lead a life like mine and you're under constant pressure to keep the bodies coming.

Some of those who died were innocent victims. Some were only getting what they deserved. Mostly

I kill men. The one time I killed a woman, it cost me a lot of grief. I dressed it up to make it look like an accident, but it was entirely deliberate—her loss was indispensable to the advancement of the story, so she had to die.

Perhaps at this point I should say that I am not an inherently violent person. My childhood was not spent torturing caterpillars. My mother was not killed in a bizarre sex slaying on a vacant lot in Pasadena. My inner demons keep mainly to themselves. I would never dream of stabbing someone over and over again in the eye with a shard of broken glass then kicking him until his spleen came out of his ears, no matter how much he might happen to deserve it. I didn't deliberately set out to become a serial killer. My homicidal rampage began entirely innocently, but it is a well-known fact that these things have a tendency to get out of hand. One thing leads to another and God knows where it will all end. Death has a life of its own.

It all began when I decided to write a novel. At the time, I didn't know much about the literature game, so I thought I'd start somewhere on the fringe and work my way towards the centre, picking things up as I went along. Eventually, I felt I'd figured out enough to write the Great Australian Novel and win the Peter Carey Prize for Best New Tim Winton. Crime fiction seemed a good place to start. It is a second-rate literary form, a hot bed of low expectations, so its appeal was obvious. For a brief moment I considered trying my hand at fantasy—but there's only so low a man can be expected to stoop.

Precisely because it makes no great literary claims for itself, crime fiction takes a lot of performance pressure off the would-be novelist. Free from the need to produce lapidary sentences and profound ruminations, the writer can get on with the job of taking the reader for a ride. But contemporary crime takes in a lot of territory and I wasn't quite sure where to begin. So I started in the usual place—by killing somebody.

My victim was a Turkish foreman in a meat-packing works in Broadmeadows. I locked him in a freezer until he expired, then stuffed his snap-frozen carcass between the pallets of spring lamb. His job was simply to get the ball rolling, to precipitate the ensuing action. He had a name but little in the way of a life history. That would come later, uncovered in the course of the story. All that mattered for the moment was the fact that he had met an untimely death and there was clearly more to the situation than met the eye of the relevant authorities.

I got the idea from my own experience. Once as a teenager, when I was working a school-holiday job, my workmates locked me in a freezer until I turned blue and began to shake uncontrollably. It was all jolly good fun, a bit of a lark, but it sort of stuck in my mind.

With a corpse suitably furnished and puzzle successfully posited, it was time for the protagonist to arrive.

In accordance with the inexorable logic of crime fiction, a suspicious death summons forth the sleuth. In most crime fiction, the killer-catcher is acting in a professional capacity. They are a representative of those institutions of society charged with the task of investigating crimes—a police officer, a coroner, a forensic pathologist or whatever. Their mission is sanctioned and supported by the apparatus and resources of the state. The investigator acts on behalf of the rest of us to seek the truth and ensure that justice is enacted.

Alternatively, the sleuth might be a private detective, a hired specialist, a gumshoe. He might be a twenty-dollar-a-day professional, a Philip Marlowe hanging his shingle for the passing trade. Operating on the fringes of the law, the gumshoe doesn't so much solve crimes as turn over rocks, setting in motion a train of events which might, or might not, reveal the truth. This process is facilitated by asking unwelcome questions and being struck over the head from behind, knocked unconscious and waking up in a puddle of piss.

The protagonist might also be an inspired amateur, a Miss Marple who treats murder as an intellectual puzzle, a mystery to be solved, a brainteaser. Such a character proves her mental and moral mettle by penetrating the significance of the fact that the pistol shot was concealed by the striking of the dinner gong by the butler, whose footprints outside the conservatory window can only be explained by young Reggie Fernacker-Clakke's sudden

interest in Eunice Crabapple's collection of rare Lepi-
doptera.

Take your pick: forensic procedural, gumshoe, cosy,
gangster—in crime fiction *par excellence*, one writer's
meat is another writer's fast-acting, almost-undetectable
poison derived from a rare plant found only in a lost
valley in the Hindu Kush. Whatever shape they might
happen to take, detectives are usually driven by easily
deciphered intentions. In police procedurals, the investigators are government functionaries, with all the
organisational complications that entails. Murder is
antisocial and its victims have rights, including full
access to the latest in electron microscopy and DNA
matching. Detection is a team effort and the individual investigators are there to provide the psychological
dimensions and the personal quirks.

Over the course of crime fiction's 150-odd-year
history, the protagonist has evolved and multiplied
into myriad forms. The shambolic homicide dick with
whisky on his breath and soup stains on his tie has
transmogrified into the female forensic pathologist in a
Chanel suit. Sherlock Holmes has become a traditionally
sized African lady from Botswana and the hard-boiled
Philip Marlowe is now a feisty goil from Noo Joisey or
a half-Danish, half-Inuit Marxist glaciologist. The job
descriptions, jurisdictions, gender and methodologies are
continuously changing, but the fundamental structure
persists—discover the crime, untangle the facts, winnow

the suspects, plumb the motives, test the alibis, apprehend the perpetrator, avenge the wrong and beat the clock. Whether amateur or professional, the habitual crime-solver is inured, if not hardened, by familiarity with the grisly details. Inspector Rex, for example, takes homicide in his stride. Ritual disembowelment one minute, a ham roll the next.

It all seems pretty straightforward, but at my first foray into the genre, I began by making a serious category error. It was a mistake which has dogged me ever since. Instead of employing a member of the killer-catching community as my protagonist, I gave the job to a rank novice called Murray Whelan, a minder, political fixer, hopeless romantic and inadvertent detective.

Wondering what an ordinary bloke might do if he began to suspect that a murder had gone undetected, that a death which had been quickly dismissed as an industrial accident was actually the result of foul play, and that somebody was getting away with it, I came up with a self-starter protagonist—an everyman equipped with no brief to investigate, no forensic expertise and no real evidence. And by way of motivation, I gave him not a copper's world-weary determination or a gumshoe's tarnished code of honour, but a mish-mash of nosiness, scepticism, loyalty, sense of justice and, when the baddie eventually comes at him with a sharpened screwdriver, pants-shitting terror.

Despite these fundamental design flaws, my accidental

hero stumbled onward, uncovering clues and upsetting the furniture. By the end of the book, the body count was a modest two. The victims, to a greater or lesser extent, deserved what they got. No innocents were harmed. No evil greater than greed was unmasked. Murray Whelan, having come face to face with murder, was physically shaken but not existentially stirred. Actually, it all worked out rather well. By that, I mean the book got published.

But a taste for murder, once acquired, is not easily shaken off. Hercules Poirot didn't stop at just one victim, nor Philip Marlowe, nor Cliff Hardy or John Rebus. No sooner had my bloke settled back into a semblance of normal life than another body popped up. That's the other thing about crime fiction. Once word gets around that you've got blood on your hands, you're expected to live up to your reputation. I was now duty bound to start offing people at regular intervals. I must become a serial killer.

Things soon began to get seriously out of hand. The death rate took a steep upward turn. From two bodies in my first book, I went to five in the second. I took a young painter with a complicated past, got him drunk and drowned him in the ornamental moat of an art gallery. I then pushed a harmless old queen down a steep riverbank. And soon after I got a gun. It's not hard to do. There are a lot more of them around than most people realise. And once I had a gun, people started to get shot.

For a while there, it looked like my bumbler would be lucky to escape with his life. Eventually, of course, the villain got his comeuppance, but only after a long trail of corpses had been delivered to the morgue.

By novel number three, I was facing a new pressure. Pace wasn't matching productivity. I wasn't killing fast enough. My American publisher complained that it took almost 100 pages to get to the first fatality. Why the long lead-up? In *Red Harvest*, Dashiell Hammett had killed 28 people by Chapter 5. I'd barely managed three—or was it four? I'd been concentrating on neither numbers nor speed but method. I started with bare hands and worked my way up to a javelin.

By the end of book four, the bodies were really starting to pile up. I ran over the first victim with a semi-trailer during a torrential pre-dawn rainstorm. I did this in order to eliminate crime-scene forensics as a plot element and leave the coppers baffled. Forensics are a bitch and the more baffled the gendarmes, the more room for manoeuvre. I then shot a truckie on the side of a country road and left a fake suicide note beside his body. This was a direct consequence of the protagonist sticking his big bib in the wrong place and exacerbating an already hairy situation. This further compounded my hapless hero's expanding repertoire of motives. As well as a natural tendency to want to right wrongs, he must also clear his name and get revenge on the bastards who offed his truckie mate.

In general we humans like to think that the motives for murder are fairly straightforward. Psychopaths do it because they're batshit crazy. Sociopaths do it because they don't give a shit. Other motives are equally easy to understand. They are derived from our most common human emotions—fear, pride, envy, anger, greed, lust and all the other deadly sins except sloth (few people are ever killed in a frenzy of unbridled sloth). Personally, I'm somewhat inclined to the view that as a motivating factor, motive is overrated. In a lot of premeditated murders, it seems to me, there is very little meditation, pre or post. At one point, I killed a family friend in a blind rage fuelled by anabolic steroids. Not only was there no real motive behind it, there was no subsequent memory. I got the idea from a real case. This idea of a motive being unnecessary doesn't just apply to murder. As Mailer or Roth or Hemingway or one of those guys once famously said, the motive for writing a novel is to write a novel.

In the contemporary crime novel an element of unresolved sexual tension is more or less obligatory. The protagonist must not only collar the killer, he must also nail the girl . . . or boy . . . or cat. It's a multi-gendered world out there, folks, and the electricity must be taken into account. And when you murder the love interest, you really ramp up the stakes. Which brings me back to the woman I mentioned earlier, the one whose convenient demise caused me grief. She was an innocent victim, collateral damage in a shootout between police and two prison escapees. She was one of my better creations, at least as far as my hero was concerned. He loved her. Which is precisely why I killed her.

In that particular book, the bullets are whistling by page three. I saw off a man's ear and feed it to a dog. There's a fight to the death in a dinghy. The cops arrive in a blaze of gunfire. It's all very cathartic. Every new book demands fresh blood, but suitable victims are not always easy to find. In the case of my most recent novel (I use the word 'recent' in the ironic sense), the suspicious death is decades old. The detection is half-arsed. The sexual tension is peripheral to the case. The only potentially violent character is overcome in a flurry of activity a few pages from the end. The issue at stake is a dead man's posthumous reputation. It wasn't really a murder anyway.

Still, they called it crime fiction, so that's what it must be. Which tends to take the pressure off a bit, I'm pleased to say. Murder can be exhausting and it's nice to ease back from time to time. But then, inevitably, you begin to feel a certain hankering.

Now where did I leave that axe?

MY RULES

There are no fucking rules. There are only fucking examples. Read some fucking books. Broaden your vocabulary. 'Fuck' can function as most parts of speech, but that doesn't mean you should limit yourself. Have a concept. Do your research. Don't procrastinate. Find inspiration. Believe in yourself. Steal. Use spellcheck. Think about all the possibilities. Persist. Get a proper thesaurus. If it doesn't work, start again. Learn from your mistakes. Get over yourself. Start as close to the end as possible. Make me care.

FIVE MUST-READS

1. The Big Sleep *by Raymond Chandler*

2. Miami Blues *by Charles Willeford*

3. The Friends of Eddie Coyle *by George V. Higgins*

4. Skintight *by Carl Hiaasen*

5. Miss Smilla's Feeling for Snow *by Peter Høeg*

Shane Maloney *is the creator of the bestselling Australian crime series, the Murray Whelan novels:* Stiff, The Brush-Off, Nice Try, The Big Ask, Something Fishy *and* Sucked In. *He is a winner of the Ned Kelly Award for Best Crime Fiction and recipient of the Australian Crime Writers Association Lifetime Achievement Award.*

THE THREE C'S

by Marele Day

I have walked through abandoned railway tunnels, been to the morgue, to police headquarters, into seedy nightclubs and drunk my fair share of whisky—all in the name of crime writing, but even a seemingly mundane task like buying a piece of office furniture can take on a heightened reality when you're a crime writer.

I was looking for a two-drawer timber filing cabinet and spent a couple of days visiting office furniture suppliers, new and second-hand, to no avail. I systematically went through the *Yellow Pages* with not much luck either. I dialled the second-last number on the list.

'You don't see many timber filing cabinets nowadays,' said a voice that sounded genuinely apologetic. There was a pause, an almost furtive pause. 'Could I interest you in a credenza?'

I paused, wondering if he was propositioning me. 'Credenza' is such a luscious, curly, opulent word; even saying it was something of an erotic experience. *Credenza.* Was it Italian for tumescence, some euphemism for the act of sexual congress? A crescendo, a climax accompanied by music? Maybe business was slow and he was bored. I was at the end of my list. I couldn't afford to treat this as an obscene phone call. Besides, I reminded myself, I was the one who'd called him.

'Excuse me, a *credenza*?'

'It's a low cabinet type of thing, timber, with a filing drawer either end.'

My nose started quivering. 'I'll be there in ten minutes.'

I walked into the second-hand store, in an unassuming, some would say sleazy, part of town. On display were metal filing cabinets, computer desks and other office furniture, but nothing fitting the description given to me by the man on the phone. Come to think of it, where was he? In these surroundings I expected to see a chap wearing a grey cardigan with patches at the elbows, who had odd personal habits. But the person who came out of the back room was young, energetic and ready to take a chance.

'Hi, how can I help you?'

'I've come about the credenza.'

'Ah, yes,' he said breezily. 'Right this way.'

We squeezed past chairs and desks till we reached

a long, low cabinet, oak by the look of it, with a deep drawer either end. Above each of these was a shallow one for stationery, and in between a cupboard area with sliding doors. It was about two metres long but no more than a metre high, just perfect for the space under my windows. This was so much more than a filing cabinet.

'I'll take it,' I said, and went home to vacuum the space where it was to stand.

That afternoon it was delivered by two hefty chaps who grunted and groaned but finally got it through the door and into place.

'Hope you don't plan on moving house,' said one of them. 'No-one's going to want to shift that.' (I did move, by the way, and the credenza came with me.)

When the delivery guys left, I gave it a dust and a polish and proceeded to fill the drawers. I placed a vase of sunflowers on the newly acquired horizontal space. And that, I thought, was that. But it was not.

When I should have been writing, I sat staring at the credenza. How did this functional, no-nonsense piece of furniture get such an exotic name? I grabbed an etymological dictionary and discovered that in Borgian days, when poisoning was an art, an Italian nobleman's meals were placed on a sideboard and tasted by a servant before being presented to the noble. If the servant didn't die or get sick, it was safe for his master to eat. From this practice the sideboard came to be called a credenza, meaning 'belief or confidence', no doubt from the belief and confidence it gave the noble, not the servant.

Having lived my life blissfully unaware of this piece of furniture with such dark origins, it then seemed to pop up everywhere. A friend in Melbourne confessed that she'd seen credenzas in the works of other crime novelists. Sue Grafton in *I Is for Innocent*:

> All the furniture was upholstered in white and oversize: big plump sofas, massive armchairs, the glass coffee table as large as a double-bed mattress. On a ponderous credenza, there was a bowl filled with wooden apples as big as softballs.

Patricia Cornwell in *Cruel and Unusual*:

> Directly behind my chair was an oak credenza I had found years earlier in the state's surplus warehouse. Its drawers had locks, making it a perfect repository for my pocketbook and active cases that were unusually sensitive.

When I found myself imagining that my oak credenza might be the very one used by Kay Scarpetta, I realised I'd lost all sense of proportion. The credenza is the repository for the story material, not the story itself, although its acquisition has parallels with writing. What you want is not always what you get. Often when you start the research you don't know what you'll discover, what the eventual story will be. My intention was to buy a filing cabinet. I ended up with something that performed that function but was a far more interesting creation. The writer must be alert to the possibilities that present themselves.

My writing process is the same, whether writing crime or those individual novels that are lumped together as literary fiction. Categories make life easier for a bookseller, but the distinctions between one genre and another are minimal from the writer's point of view. There are the same concerns with character, structure and pacing, language, ways of engaging the reader.

I normally do three drafts, and each of those drafts has a different function. Basically the first draft is for myself, to get ideas on paper. The second draft is for the characters, to tell their story as best I can. The third draft is for the reader, to focus on language in ways that make the experience of reading pleasurable.

Of course, there's more to constructing a novel than the words on the page. There's also the 'couch work'. My office furniture is a triumvirate of c's: credenza, computer and couch. Everything ends up in the credenza but begins on the couch. Recently re-upholstered, the couch has been with me even longer than the credenza. It is where Claudia Valentine was conceived. To the casual eye it appears as if I'm having a rest when on the couch, but in fact this is where the invisible work takes place, the vast proportion below the writing line—designing and building the world of the novel, conjuring up its inhabitants, thinking about what they might do.

Not only is it the place for daydreaming, doing research in the imagination, it is also the work station for the first draft. Like Robert Louis Stevenson, Mark Twain and Truman Capote, at this stage I write lying down. Capote described himself as a 'completely horizontal writer'. Quirkier still, Dame Edith Sitwell was in the habit of lying in an open coffin before beginning the day's writing. Benjamin Franklin wrote in the bath, and Edgar Allan Poe supposedly wrote with a cat on his shoulder (possibly to keep the ravens away).

The first draft is written longhand, in hardcover foolscap notebooks. I wrote two of the Claudia Valentine novels (*The Last Tango of Dolores Delgado* and *The Disappearances of Madalena Grimaldi*) straight onto the computer, but found it to be an unsatisfying experience. I missed the tactility of pen and paper, of hand-shaping the words. The flow of handwriting comes from a different part of the brain than the on/off movement of tapping on a keyboard. Periodically I move to the computer and key in what I've written, so that if the worst should happen—theft or fire—there is a copy. Of course, any thief with an IQ higher than room temperature would take the computer rather than an exercise book full of almost illegible writing.

In the triumvirate of c's the computer is the go-between—a processor of the ideas and words. Although I've stuck with the same couch and credenza, there has been a succession of computers, starting with an Amstrad, my favourite, which in the early days had its own software—Locoscript—producing green words on a black screen. A couple of bulky PCs followed, then the suite of laptops.

In the first draft I'm trying to construct scenes and events, settings and various locations, the beginnings of characterisation, a general tone, etc. Though I don't necessarily know what's going to happen, I usually have some idea of an initiating incident that will propel the narrative—a murder, the detective taking the case.

Everything is very loose and flexible. In the first layer of words on the page I often write notes to myself, put in bits that sound like good ideas but may be in the wrong place. Rather than looking for the phrase or image that precisely conveys the idea (and I can spend hours deliberating over a comma), I write the same thing three or four ways. I aim for a thousand words a day and never read over what I've done the day before so that my ineptitude or clumsiness doesn't dishearten me. First drafts are exactly that. They're not meant to be the final version. Things will change, improve.

I don't revise at this stage either. It seems pointless to polish a piece of writing that may change radically or not end up in the final draft at all. In the beginning

I'm trying to put down all the elements of the novel that will make the whole, as well as moving towards a finishing point.

I may have an intention for the novel before I begin—an idea I want to explore—but it's not till at least three-quarters of the way through the first draft, when enough words have accumulated, that I discover what the novel *wants* to be, what it's really about. From that moment my original intentions become irrelevant.

I guess another writer might consider my first draft to be note-taking or the basic outline before the actual writing starts, but I find it agonising to plot and plan beforehand. When I first began writing a novel, I tried to create a blueprint or outline, but found the process so creatively stifling that I gave myself permission to proceed without much of a plan, to meander into unknown territory, to travel without a map.

I have a 'rest' (not on the couch) between first and second drafts, a few weeks, to let the material cool and solidify. Then I read through that first draft, uploading it all back into my brain, because while some of the material is fairly recent, other sections have been written more than a year before. Now I see possibilities that weren't evident at the time of writing. Unless something is obvious, I don't make corrections during the reading process, but I do mark up paragraphs—double lines for *definitely needs attention*, squiggly lines for *not quite right*. I'm engaged in what we might call 'passive receptivity', a kind of meditative state, in which you 'listen' to what the text is saying.

Before I begin the second draft, I determine what the principal scenes are and the best way to arrange them, putting them on a whiteboard in point form. The large surface of the whiteboard allows the overall structure to be seen at a glance. In the second draft I look at the logical implications of the story, the cause and effect between events. This is where I work out the rate of flow of information, the building of suspense and intrigue, the delicate balance of giving enough information to keep the reader interested without giving too much away. I move bits and pieces around like players on a board or actors on a stage: some information given later should be given earlier and vice versa. It's the art of seduction—wooing the reader into the story.

Again I'm not paying particular attention to the language but to the macro elements—structure, pacing, characterisation—what motivates characters, their secret hopes and fears, are they fully fleshed, can we hear distinctive narrative voices, does the detail convey the large patterns of the novel?

The third draft focuses on the words themselves, the micro level. Here I will pin down the exact phrase and image, pay attention to the poetic function of language, the rhythm, flow, make sure the style reflects content. I read this draft aloud to hear those rhythms, the beats and pauses. Are sentences too long, short, is there enough variety in sentence structure to avoid the monotone? Are there opportunities to enrich the text without skewing it?

I had never read any crime fiction before writing *The Life and Crimes of Harry Lavender*. The original motivation was to write a book about Sydney. From the beginning of my writing career, 'place' has always been a source of inspiration. I started writing when I started travelling. Instead of taking photographs I wrote a few words about the places I visited. Eventually the words became poems and eventually, when I became interested not only in language but in telling stories, I wanted to try my hand at a novel. For that I needed to practise writing plot. A detective story seemed to kill these two birds with the one stone—both a plot-strong genre and a vehicle for showing the city.

I hadn't read any crime fiction but I had seen a lot of film noir, and wanted to have a detective who talked the tough talk.

> *'So many guns around town and so few brains.'* (The Big Sleep)

> *'You drinking that stuff this early?'*
> *'Listen, darling, when you drink as much as I do, you gotta start early.'* (Cry Danger)

Oh, and why not a female detective? This was how the first Claudia Valentine novel came about, but there's a prehistory too, a French connection that can be tracked back a decade to my student days at Sydney University: three autobiographical works of French writer, Albertine Sarrazin, that piqued my interest in life on the wrong side of the law. Sarrazin was street-wise, talked the tough talk (*en français bien sûr*) having spent a quarter of her short life in a remand home and prison.

French studies also provided exposure to structuralism and semiotics (then radical and refreshing approaches) that focused on how stories were assembled, examining their architecture. My mother was a bookbinder. As a child I knew how books were put together, spines stitched, endpapers pasted to inside covers, etc, but not how the stories in the books were made. I assumed that what I was reading on the page was a natural part of the paper, like the grain in timber.

Crime fiction was influential in shaping the works of the French New Novelists such as Alain Robbe-Grillet, Nathalie Sarraute and Claude Simon, as well as narratologist Tzvetan Todorov, who called the genre the novel form par excellence. There is a 'mystery' in all narratives—what happens, who makes it happen, when, where, why is this story being told? The writer provides subtle clues that should eventually answer these questions.

We read fiction to know what it is to be human, to experience, through this parallel universe, the lives of others. A novelist is a storyteller as well as a writer, and storytellers have been part of our experience since humans developed the ability to communicate with each other. We are creatures with senses and we seek sensation, ideally something that vicariously takes us into dangerous terrain but keeps us physically safe. There's comfort in the knowledge that while the protagonist of the story is hanging off a cliff somewhere, or in a pit of snakes or the throes of their own worst nightmare, we are sitting around a cosy fire, tucked up in bed, or lying by the pool with a long cool drink.

Good crime fiction is what every novel should be— great writing, an exploration of the human condition, reflections on the world around us, with a mystery at the very heart. In essence, a ripping good yarn.

MY RULES

I have just the one: keep readers interested, keep them turning the page, and in the end, pay them off for their attention.

FIVE MUST-READS

1. **This Is How** by M.J. Hyland

2. **Get Shorty** by Elmore Leonard

3. **Written on the Skin** by Liz Porter

4. **The Little Black and White Book of Film Noir** by Peg Thompson & Saeko Usukawa (editors)

5. **Murder in Pastiche** by Marion Mainwaring

Marele Day *is the author of eight novels including the Claudia Valentine series, which has become a classic of Australian crime writing and features a feisty inner-city gumshoe living in Sydney. Marele is the editor of* How to Write Crime *and recipient of several awards, including the Ned Kelly Lifetime Achievement Award.*

WHAT ELSE IS THERE TO DO?

by Peter Corris

I met David Malouf at some writing function and, simply for something to say, asked him if he was writing just then.

'What else is there to do?' he said.

It's a bit like that with me. After writing virtually every day for over 30 years, it has become something like breathing—stop it and I'd die.

I am addicted to writing. Like a smoker who claims not to be addicted to nicotine but to the gestures, the cigarette selection, the lighting, the ashing, the stubbing out. I am addicted to the process: turning on the computer, getting the file up, tapping the keys, saving, storing on the memory stick. But just as the smoker is kidding him- or herself about the nature of the dependency, I have to admit that my dependency is also emotional and psychological.

As a child I longed to be good at sport. I wasn't. I was a better than average tennis player but 'way short' (as my seven-year-old grandson would say) of being really good. It was the same with athletics, and when I wept after being hit on the nose in a boxing match at the YMCA the instructor said, 'This isn't for you, son.'

I can't sing in tune. My attempts to play the guitar were lamentable failures. I'm too inhibited to dance properly unless released from the shackles by alcohol. So what can I do?

At primary school I was first with my hand up to give a morning talk. My talks would be loosely based on fact but much embellished. Stories, in fact. When I was in the higher grades and a teacher was absent, I was the one picked to read to a lower class and sometimes extemporise a story. This facility didn't make me popular, but at least caused me to be noticed.

And so it went on. My strong subjects were History and English where I could write, teasing my own meaning out of the question and so impressing the examiners. I did an Honours degree in History and English at the University of Melbourne and topped the class list. My MA and PhD theses weren't notable for the depth of their analysis, but were found 'readable'. As a result, when I gave up on academia the only other possible profession open to me appeared to be journalism.

My love of, and ability at, reading and writing stem, I believe, from a wish to escape from a dreary, emotionally undernourished childhood. No neglect, no ill treatment, just a stifling atmosphere of secular Puritanism that damaged, luckily not permanently, my social and sexual self-confidence. I escaped into books and a deep well opened beneath me, filled with stories, my frustrations and fragilities and the knack of a vivid and fertile imagination. I've drawn on that well, and my more satisfying adult experiences, for all of my writing life.

My first ventures into fiction, when still an academic or in my early days as a journalist, were short stories. These were very conventional efforts, vaguely academic in tone, somewhat modelled on the stories of Somerset Maugham. I got regular rejection slips with helpful comments such as, 'No' or 'Not for us'.

Maugham was a favourite of mine, but success seemed not to lie in that direction. I tried turning my doctoral thesis on the Solomon Islands labour trade into a historical novel, my favourite kind of fiction. Called *Brown Sugar*, the contrived narrative and artificial mix of sex and politics was rejected by a dozen or more publishers.

The hard-boiled private detectives of Raymond Chandler, Dashiell Hammett and Ross MacDonald appealed to me strongly. Holed up in a cheap hotel in San Francisco in 1971, waiting for money from Australia, I bought ten or more of these books for a few cents each, devoured them, and it dawned on me that Sydney resembled San Francisco in certain ways and would be a good setting for an Australian private eye. The idea lay dormant for a few years until my break with academia and after the failure of the short stories.

In Sydney, living hand-to-mouth as a freelance journalist with three children and a mortgage, I wrote what would become *The Dying Trade* in a matter of weeks. Mainstream publishers and small presses rejected it outright. They seemed to think that Australian crime readers were only interested in stories set in London, New York or LA. They should have known better.

Australian readers have always responded well to local settings in historical novels and the war and romance genres. The first bestseller here was Fergus Hume's *The Mystery of a Hansom Cab*, set in Melbourne, and the novels of Arthur Upfield were popular, with their outback settings, in the 1930s and 1940s. There was no reason why the urban detective story shouldn't succeed here.

This stiff publisher resistance to a locally set crime novel was only broken by luck. I was writing book reviews for Elizabeth Riddell, then literary editor of the *Australian*. Jim Hall, a former editor of that paper and a friend of Elizabeth's, had been appointed to create an Australian fiction list for the American publisher McGraw-Hill. Jim Hall was a fan of the hard-boiled Californian private eye and Elizabeth suggested I send him *The Dying Trade*.

The McGraw-Hill venture was virtually still-born, publishing only two books, but mine was one of them. *The Dying Trade* received favourable reviews and was picked up by Pan Books as a paperback. By then I'd written another Cliff Hardy book and had a third almost finished because I enjoyed writing them so much and found it so easy. Now, 37 Hardy books have been published and another is ready for publication in 2013.

In addition to the Hardy books, I've written three novels featuring a witness-protection officer and one true crime book, *Mad Dog: William Cyril Moxley and the Moorebank killings*. Despite what you may have heard, crime can pay. That, of course, is a strong motivating factor apart from writing as a personal solace and an enjoyment. Readers and some writers sometimes imagine that we do this for love and 'art', but there is also the need to make a living. Through the 1980s and 1990s I consistently published more than one book a year, often three and once four. These were in different genres and included anthologies on boxing and golf, as well as histories and short stories and four 'as told to' autobiographies. In recent times two books a year has been my usual output. Publishers' advances are not large, the flow of royalties can be sluggish and sales are shrinking. Only the money coming in from the Public and Educational Lending Right schemes has enabled me to live by writing alone. I consider myself very fortunate to have achieved that.

I'm doubly fortunate in that I haven't found the production of this body of work difficult. When writing the Hardy books, the Crawley spy novels, the Browning picaresque stories and the Dunlop witness-protection books, my usual work pattern has been to write twice a day for about an hour each time. I write from about 11 a.m. to noon and from 5 p.m. to 6 p.m.

I revealed my writing routine on radio once and got into trouble with a friend whose son wasn't performing well at school. The distressed father said something to him like, 'How can you expect to be a success when you don't work hard at school?' The kid said, 'Peter Corris is a success and he only works two hours a day.' Of course this isn't the whole story. I'm writing all the time—thinking of things, rehearsing dialogue, observing people and places. Putting words on the page is the very last part of the writing process.

When I actually sit down to work I find enough material to advance the story. I don't count the words as I write, but I seem to know when enough is satisfying. At the end of each chapter I count the words to give me a sense of how the book is progressing. This is necessary because I don't plan the books at all; I simply let each writing session build on the last until I feel that it's time to shape the material towards a convincing ending. Then some forward planning comes into play. It's an edgy way to work with the ever-present fear that the flow might stop, but so far so good.

The process is entirely different with the historical novels, the nonfiction and the 'as told to' autobiographies. These involve more research, taking notes and referencing material, keeping track of generations, dates and time. It requires many hours working in libraries and archives and, more recently, on the web, before I can sit down at my desk and begin writing. It's more taxing—maintaining consistency of tone, avoiding contradictions and repetition, presenting facts—but just as enjoyable and in some ways more so because of my deeper involvement.

My daughters claim that, in days gone by when they were young and at home, they would occasionally hear me bang the desk and shout, 'Great stuff!' I can't deny it. I get enormous satisfaction when I see on the screen an acute description, a well-turned phrase or a good joke.

I don't like working under pressure, to deadlines or to make good on an advance. For this reason I have only once taken an advance for fiction not yet written. This was for the package of three witness-protection books. I wrote them in nine weeks, one after another, to rid myself of the feeling of being *obliged* to write. That exercise required a fair bit of whisky. Otherwise, with fiction, I take an advance only when the completed manuscript has been accepted.

I have never workshopped or taught creative writing because I wouldn't know how. The great golfer Peter Thompson was once asked why he'd never written a 'how to' book. He said he couldn't because all he'd have to say was, 'Take the club straight back and swing it straight through.' It's something like that with me. When asked for advice about writing all I can say is, 'Imitate the manner of the writer you most admire using your own material.'

Until I was into my stride, the early Hardy novels were pastiches of Chandler and MacDonald; the early Crawley books imitated Len Deighton, while the Browning stories copied George MacDonald Fraser's *Flashman*.

I can offer no tips about creating characters, devising plots, generating suspense or anything else. These things just come to me instinctively. As I'm writing I see and hear what is happening and I put it on the page. Sometimes I can compose quite long passages in my head while out walking or sitting drinking coffee and reproduce them more or less exactly in the next writing session. I never re-read what I've written and very seldom revise a word or a phrase. Just occasionally I sense a flatness or awkwardness and sit back for a moment to rework the passage.

Beginnings are easy for the detective stories. The client has a problem. This problem comes to me from that deep well I mentioned earlier, or from something I've seen or read or heard. This simplicity of approach is not to say that I'm not aware of certain techniques or tricks. I seem to have had these in my repertoire from the start, presumably from having read popular fiction in different styles for 30 years before I started writing. Unconsciously the methods soaked into my bones. I'm always aware of the balance between narrative description and dialogue. Too much of either can kill the story. Chandler, though somewhat dated now by racism and sexism, was a master of this.

Similarly, I very deliberately in my fiction make sure that the chapter ends on a note that impels the reader forward. Subtly sometimes, blatantly at others, whatever I deem appropriate. Beyond that, and the shaping of the story towards a satisfying conclusion, I do very little other than one thing adopted from Ernest Hemingway— I always leave off writing knowing what's going to come next. The result is that I'm always anxious to get back to work and never have a reluctance to do so. The maxim that the longest journey for a writer is from the armchair to the desk has no meaning for me. I am a self-starter.

Since I started writing I've never had to abort a short story or a novel or make drastic changes in their structure. Journalist and friend Stuart Coupe once embarked on a biography of me which, thankfully, he never completed. Along the way he compared published Hardy books with the manuscript deposited in the State Library of New South Wales and found them very substantially the same. This is proof of how much I dislike rewriting and dread major changes.

I don't write second drafts, but my wife, Jean Bedford, is my first reader and she 'civilises' the manuscript, drawing attention to slips, repetitions, dull spots, inappropriate editorialising and typos. Jean has also given me titles and, at least once, steered me off a faulty plot path.

I also owe a debt to the publishers' readers and editors who further refine the work, pointing out factual errors, suggesting more felicitous expressions, always judiciously, knowing how reluctant I am to make changes.

Like most writers (though not all, I gather), I owe a great debt to agents I've had over the years, particularly Rosemary Creswell. I dislike reading contracts, much less negotiating them, and the work my agents have done in furthering my career has been immense. This was brought home to me recently when I happened to give a contract more than the usual cursory glance. I noticed a clause stating that the publisher reserved the right to reject the submitted manuscript. I told my present agent, Gaby Naher, that I'd never seen this before. 'That's because,' she said somewhat sharply, 'you've always had an agent in your corner. Any agent worth his or her salt will have that clause taken out.'

Of course there have been disappointments. I've written eight historical novels, none of which has been as successful as I'd hoped. One attracted a very large advance from the publisher with a plan to publish simultaneously in the United Kingdom and the United States. UK publication never happened, while the American edition was a trashy-looking paperback that sank without a trace. I still think some of my best writing is in these books, particularly in the now totally forgotten *The Brothers Craft*.

Another disappointment came when I signed on to help actor Bill Hunter do his autobiography. I liked Bill, met him a number of times and taped the interviews. Invariably we met in pubs, in Queensland, northern New South Wales or Sydney, where Bill smoked many cigarettes and drank many schooners. He told me stories about his time as a stockman and as a swimming champion. He had rubbed shoulders in London with one of the great train robbers and John Lennon. He'd worked with Aboriginal people in the bush, been arrested and jailed briefly. He'd woken up in Perth after a drinking session in Sydney with no idea how he got there. He'd played leading roles in three hit films in a row: *Strictly Ballroom*, *Muriel's Wedding* and *Priscilla, Queen of the Desert* and won many acting awards.

It was fabulous material and I had hopes of a best-seller, but the manuscript finished up five or six thousand words short. I sent the printout, my tape recorder and some cassettes to Bill, and asked him to talk to passages he could expand. I waited but heard nothing from him. I wrote and got no answer. His agent told the publisher Bill had withdrawn from the project and paid back his and my advance and compensated me for the loss of the tape recorder. I heard indirectly that when Bill saw the stuff in cold, hard print he realised that some of what he'd told me wasn't true and that others would know.

The success of the Cliff Hardy character swamped the other serial characters, Browning and Crawley. I would have liked to continue with these characters and had ideas for further outings for them, but when quite good reviews took on a tone of 'this isn't a Cliff Hardy book but nevertheless . . .' sales dipped and the publishers lost interest.

I am very aware of my limitations. I have no profound insights into the human condition, no passions apart from an intense dislike of religion and conservative politics. Journalist and editor Rosemary Sorenson once said to me, 'Peter, you're such a lazy writer.' I think she meant that if I took more time and tried harder I could write something more substantial. I think she was mistaken.

It annoys me when popular writers like Lee Child, Matthew Reilly and Bryce Courtenay claim that they could write literary novels ('a superlative literary novel' was Courtenay's claim), if they chose. This is nonsense. There is a difference between their books and those, say, of Margaret Drabble and Ian McEwan. The difference is in the use of language and the thought and feeling behind it, the sensibility.

Child, Reilly and Courtenay would do well to take a leaf from Somerset Maugham's book. Maugham asserted that he was at the very front of the second rank. He sold in the millions, as the three writers named do, and, at his best, was a better writer than any of them.

MY RULES

I don't like advising or dictating. Learn from your mistakes and successes. And as I mentioned earlier, imitate the manner of the writer you most admire using your own material.

FIVE MUST-READS

1. **The Complete Short Stories of W. Somerset Maugham** *(3 vols)*

2. **The Collected Essays, Journalism and Letters of George Orwell** *(4 vols)*

3. **Why I Am Not a Christian** *by Bertrand Russell*

4. **The Big Sleep** *by Raymond Chandler*

5. **The Mayor of Casterbridge** *by Thomas Hardy*

Formerly an academic historian and a journalist, novelist **Peter Corris** *has been dubbed 'the Godfather of contemporary Australian crime-writing', having created Private Investigator Cliff Hardy, one of the most important and enduring characters in Australian popular fiction.*

I KNOW IT'S ONLY NOIR (BUT I LIKE IT)

by Lenny Bartulin

The first thing that happened was that I fell in love. *She* came along. Miss Noir. Long legs, luscious lips with that goddamn pout, flowing hair and a look that just dismissed you, that put you in your place, like somebody slicing off your legs.

'But you're just a *boy*,' she said, blowing out a plume of cool blue smoke.

From that moment I didn't want to be Samuel Beckett anymore.

Noir is timeless, like jazz, like rock'n'roll. The thrill of reading, say, *The Big Sleep* or *The Blonde on the Street Corner* or *Double Indemnity* for the first time has never left me. And apart from the stories themselves, it was the writing that blew me away: all that style, the sharp dialogue, the cynical humour, the flawless craft.

It was writing with intent and purpose, writing that delivered and gave the reader real pleasure. It had *bottom-end*. Weight. It could take you into tight bends at speed but you were never going to flip. It reminded me of being a kid again—the unadulterated joy of opening a new book, entering a completely new world, my innocence in cahoots with my imagination. I'd finally discovered what kind of writer I wanted to be. In a word: honest.

There's an early passage in the 1947 novel *The Dark Chase*, by the American writer David Goodis, that describes a man—Vanning—on the streets of a hot Manhattan night. It's really late; nobody in the city can sleep. He has stepped outside his apartment building in the hope of some relief, a breath of fresh air. We know something is up. There is pressure here along with the heat and there's no doubt that Vanning's wearing a little stress, but nothing has been explained yet. He turns the corner and a man comes up to him, asking for a light. They exchange a few words.

> 'Hot night,' the man said.
> 'Terrific.'
> 'I saw some kids diving off the docks,' the man said. 'They got the right idea.'
> 'If we did it,' Vanning said, 'people would call us crazy.'
> 'The trouble with people is they don't understand people.'

Two people, five lines, but look at the volumes in there. Noir loves people. Down-and-out people and bad people and sad people and those out there giving it a good swing of the bat. Human beings. Characters. Oh, there are lots of ideas in Noir too, about the rot inside the capitalist dream, the raw deal, the existential emptiness, the loneliness of a man or woman surrounded and bumped by millions just like them. There's plenty of serious stuff that works to cord the muscles of literary merit. But as a writer, the emphasis on character, the way that narrative is developed through dialogue and action, through making the characters *real*, was a revelation. It was as though I'd found the key to my writer-self.

That's it! I cried. That's what I like, and I'm pretty sure that's what I can do, or at least what I'm going to try to do.

For me, the novel, the barest idea for a novel, begins with the characters. If they're not real, if they're not human, there is no novel.

In a collection of essays titled *Afterwords—Novelists on their novels*, the author, Wright Morris, says, 'My talent, such as it is, finds its realisation in the creation of *characters*.' In the introduction to the collection, the editor, Thomas McCormack, picks up on this.

'This is an important thing to know about oneself,' he writes. 'Perhaps the primary task of any artist —any person—is to discover what he or she can and cannot do.'

So I found my 'thing'. And then I had to go to work.

Okay, the nitty gritty. If you want, there's staring out the window, thinking. There are long walks with a pen and notepad, waiting for inspiration to strike. And there are sleepless nights, still thinking, staring into the dark void, plenty of what my wife calls *brain burn*. These are all part of the process, but it's also where you most easily get bogged down, really good and sunk. But there's a cure: and though my past schoolteachers would be shocked to hear me say this, I have discovered the secret: *discipline*.

When Keith Richards was asked where the songs came from, he said, well, I just stick my antenna up and wait. They're all up there, he said, in the stratosphere. Sticking his antenna up meant picking up the guitar and playing, simple as that. It's no different for a writer. You play and practise. I see it as a way of getting into the zone, that necessary state of openness and flow, when you plug into the world around you. Pick up your pen or boot up the laptop, sit down and write.

Practise. Every day. It's the job of coaxing the universe around to your place. When your antenna is up, ideas come and problems are solved, the words stick. (Most of the time, anyway.) Creativity is a volatile thing, constantly changing shape and colour, like the churning, gaseous surface of Jupiter. What I discovered was that discipline helped provide me with an anchor, and showed me a path through a place where there are no maps or markers.

For many years now, I've been getting up at 4 a.m. to write. Six days a week. I kill the alarm, crawl out of bed, flip-flop into the kitchen and put the coffee on to brew. Wow, but it's quiet. Dark, too. Coffee done, I move into the office (kitchen table for many years, now a spare bedroom), switch on the computer, flick on the lamp. I'm here. Deep breath, take a sip. Start reading the bit where I left off the day before, or maybe read a paragraph or two from a favourite book, get the juices going. It could be Richard Stark or Elmore Leonard, one of Elizabeth Bishop's letters or a passage from Darwin's *The Voyage of the Beagle* (and for those of you who haven't read him, nobody uses a comma like Darwin). I don't try too hard yet, just ease on in with that first cup of coffee. It's a start, an anchor. Then, you know, you've got to nudge it a little.

I have two and a half hours, maybe three, so I get with the characters as soon as possible. See what they're doing. See what they might want to do. With a new book, it's more tentative and careful and there are lots of good manners on show. In the same way you might meet people at the pub or at a dinner party, it should start with small, easy questions, like, '*So how long have you been living in Sydney?*' You don't meet somebody for the first time and immediately start in on your 'Theory of Everything' monologue.

There's give and take, a little grin here and there, fishing with a light line out on flat water. Let's see what happens. If I'm well into a manuscript—and assuming things are hunky dory, of course—the characters direct the show more forcefully and I try to follow, sometimes sprinting to keep up with them. But at the beginning of a new book, or even earlier, when apparently non-related strands are starting to come together and look like a possible story, everything is really loose; because ideas for characters and stories and settings and plots kind of happen together, swirling in and around one another, influencing each other. Repelling each other, too.

It's impossible to tell which one comes first, so sometimes it's difficult to find an opening. It's like you're hunting butterflies with a net but there are these great bugs around too, and grasshoppers and wow, look at that bird over there. There are lots of ideas, but no form, no shape. This is a great time to try to get an early handle on things, drive a stake into the ground. Anywhere, come on. Here, look, this'll do fine. You just need to start.

I begin by asking three questions: WHO? WHERE? WHY?

My very own Holy Trinity. Who is the character? Where is the character? And why the hell are they there?

It helps to break things down. To make a jigsaw you need the pieces, and a novel needs a lot of pieces.

Who is the character?

Male or female? How old? Name? Age? Job? Married

or single? Divorced? Of course, many of these things might not even go into the story, and many of them you won't discover until you've begun writing it, but you're immediately presented with things to *test*.

Where is the character?

This adds further pieces, and immediately feeds into the first question: if the *where* is, say, an oil rig in the South China Sea, it's unlikely the *who* will be a 70-year-old widow from Mosman. Or is it? Trying to bring the scenario off could well provide you with a very interesting, *Why is she there?* So test it with a paragraph or two. Has it got legs? Is the character believable?

Mrs Swanton refused to step out of the helicopter until the blades stopped spinning. She looked out over the deck of the oil rig and saw the lashing wind and rain. There was a man in a yellow vest yelling and waving an arm at her, holding an umbrella that would any second snap inside out, but she ignored him, lost for a moment in the thought of her husband, Arthur, being swept off this very deck and into the sea, only yesterday. He'd come to inspect the rig, flown out from the rooftop of their hotel in Shanghai, where they'd been spending their fiftieth wedding anniversary. He'd said, 'Well, I'm here, and it's my rig. Why not?' He'd always been hands-on in the business. She was pleased he would be gone for the day. For 50 years, all he'd ever talked about was oil. Now that she was there on the deck herself, Mrs Swanton wondered why she'd insisted on coming to collect the body. To make sure that he really was dead?

No? Okay, we could try something else then: make Mrs Swanton 28, make it that she and 70-year-old Arthur were enjoying their *first* wedding anniversary, make it that the guy in the yellow vest turns out to be her lover, and maybe he had something to do with the old man going over the side . . .

The most important thing is that you're *moving* the story along. That's your job as a writer. And to my mind, believable characters best carry the burden of the narrative arc.

Crafting the story through the creation and exploration of characters is exciting and creatively satisfying, and if this is translated to the reader, your writing will have energy and power. Once characters are in motion, anything is possible. Once they're real, they can spout Nietzsche or shoot Uzis, but first they need pumping hearts and blood and muscle. They'll show you where to go . . . and they'll also tell you where you've gone wrong.

Going wrong happens a lot. The way I write relies in no small measure on faith and intuition, which naturally leads to mistakes and, at worst, to complete disasters. Faith and intuition are slow developers. They take a lot of time, and insist on bad decisions, kind of like your guts insist on 'good' bacteria. Though the pay-off can be huge, so can the cost.

I was about two-thirds of the way through my first novel when one day, just like that, the earth split open beneath my feet and I found myself plummeting into molten lava. My faith and intuition had run out of steam and I never saw it coming. I thought my book was suddenly a waste of space, absolutely terrible, and I had no idea how to finish it. These things happen, and you get through them, or you don't, but there's always something to learn, something that can feed and rejuvenate your faith and intuition, if you summon the courage to face the challenge.

That first time, I was lucky to receive a piece of good advice: *the solution is in your book*. I didn't know what it meant straightaway, but I got it eventually. The book is not the problem, but rather a map to the problem. Seeing as I wrote it, I should be able to find my way with the directions. Harder than it sounds, of course, but it's another way of breaking the thing down into the jigsaw pieces.

It's a crazy job, writing novels. Essentially you're a problem solver, but the problem is one of your own devising. *Hey, I know! I'm gonna dedicate my life to giving myself a regular goddamn headache! Is there any money in it?* As your courage grows, and as your ambition and abilities develop, so does the size of your headache. But boy, I love those headaches. And you have to, because nobody else will.

Noir is naturally lean. There's no excess fat, no wobble, no doughy flanks. It's writing that is road-hardened, nicotine-stained and laced with liquor. Describing the writing of Jim Thompson, Barry Hannah once said, 'Thompson writes like a haunch of raw beef slammed on a table.'

This style clicked with me in a big way, it spoke to me on more levels than any other writing ever had before. Noir came along at a crucial time, when my mind had been straying. I had been thinking about what it would be like to have a novel written, rather than actually writing one. Worst of all, I'd forgotten how to be a reader, how to slip into a book like a hot bath, and that alone nearly sank me. Noir changed all that. In short, it saved me.

So at four in the morning, I'm the man with no name, the stranger in town, the guy on the dark corner trying to light his cigarette with an empty Bic when there's nobody around with a spare match. But hang on. Is that somebody coming down the street? Who could it be? Well, let me tell you a story . . .

MY RULES

1. **Read two shit-hot books and watch one shit-hot film before you begin.**

   Get fired up. Remind yourself of the pleasure of a great story . . . then write a better one.

2. Don't read more than two shit-hot books or watch more than one shit-hot film before you begin.

This could well lead to depression and make you wonder if there's any point to writing anything at all.

3. Don't keep any 'ideas for a story'.

Especially in fancy, leather-bound diaries. If they're worth anything, you'll remember them. And if you don't, they were probably best forgotten. The brain is a natural filter. Some ideas were born to be lost.

4. Read and read more and be grateful.

The imagination is a miracle. Writing is an act of thanks.

5. Words, words, words . . . don't worry about them too much.

While you're alive, you can have as many as you want. They're free. Chuck 'em about, play with them; they're your sandcastles on the beach.

6. Keep yourself out of it.

You're the writer, that's it. Apart from that, you're nobody and probably pretty fucking boring and nobody gives a shit.

7. Learn to handle rejection and neglect.

See above.

8. Do not drink more than one bottle of red wine per day.

Unless you can.

9. Remember to ask your wife how her day is going.

And try not to mention your book until she's finished telling you.

10. Do not take yourself too seriously.

One day, somebody asked my then four-year-old, 'What does your daddy do?' He answered, 'Typing.' I've got it framed on my desk.

FIVE MUST-READS
(IN NO PARTICULAR ORDER)

1. **The Big Sleep** by Raymond Chandler
2. **Jack's Return Home** by Ted Lewis
3. **The Little Friend** by Donna Tartt
4. **For Whom the Bell Tolls** by Ernest Hemingway
5. **The Fatal Shore** by Robert Hughes

Lenny Bartulin *is the author of three crime novels featuring the wisecracking purveyor of second-hand books, Jack Susko, who has a nose for trouble and an eye for the ladies.*

KEEPING IT REAL

by Liz Porter

Some true crime stories have done everything but jump out of the police notebook and demand I record them. One of the most memorable involved a parcel bomb blast in which a man was killed after opening a gift package delivered to the Adelaide home where he boarded. Decorated with kisses and love hearts and bearing the message 'from a secret admirer', the parcel had been sent, police suspected, by the victim's ex and her new lover.

Even when narrating a real event, a writer must decide how to organise the narrative. Who are the main characters? From whose point of view will the story be told? Where will it begin?

I could choose to start in the immediate aftermath of the blast or many years before when the seeds for the crime were first planted. I could investigate the child-hood and events that helped shape the psychopathic personality required to execute such a crime.

Many writers, novelists and true crime authors alike would go with the 'deadly love triangle' aspect of the above case. What extraordinary passions would drive a woman to do such a thing? And what sort of man would help her?

I asked myself these same questions when I wrote Chapter 7 of my book, *Written on the Skin: An Australian forensic casebook*. And it says something about me as a writer that my choice of protagonist was a man who would be lucky to get a walk-on role in an *Underbelly* telemovie version of the story.

I focused my attention on a mild-mannered police forensic investigator, Paul Sheldon, who was on the crime scene within 90 minutes of the blast. First he began dividing the area into a grid so that teams of police could spend the next few days collecting and sorting every fragment of twisted metal, wire and charred paper they could find on the property. Sheldon used his analysis of this material to reconstruct the bomb—made from an Australia Post pack, two tin cans, several metres of detonating cord and a battery. His next task was to figure out whether anything in the material from the blast scene might betray the identity of the bombers. His money was on the microscopic marks on the fragments of tin can, which he and his colleagues surmised were made by the cogs of an electric can-opener when it clicked under the rim of each can. But could he prove that these marks had been made by one particular appliance, such as the GE-brand opener in the kitchen of a house occupied by the father of one of the suspects?

In a series of 'test' openings of cans, Sheldon identified an appliance that left exactly the same sequences of microscopic marks as the ones observed and photographed on the bomb fragments. But so what? That wasn't proof that this opener had made the marks. Other can-openers might leave identical marks and in the same sequence.

To test this hypothesis, Sheldon collected fourteen different can-openers and undertook the laborious process of opening thousands of cans with them, photographing the indentations they made and printing the images on long, thin strips of photographic paper. He then made an eye-watering, brain-numbing 62 128 comparisons. Working by eye, he lined up these indentations against the marks made by the 'suspect' opener, against the bomb fragment samples—and against each other, plotting his results on a giant sheet of graph paper. At the joint murder trial of the victim's ex and her lover, Sheldon was able to testify that only the 'suspect' can-opener left the same marks—and in the same sequence—as the marks found on the bomb fragments. Paul Sheldon had proved that each can-opener had its own 'fingerprint'.

As a reader, I love the fictional exploits of lone macho heroes, either criminals or cops. A special 'hello' here to Lee Child's tough, sexy Jack Reacher and to Garry Disher's wily sociopath, Wyatt. But, speaking as a writer, my kind of hero is a man—or woman—like Paul Sheldon. Yes, he confesses to being 'a bit anal', which is his explanation for being able to survive such work. Yet he displays the kind of heroic qualities that I like to write about: the unsung, often unpraised virtues of persistence, doggedness, infinite patience and obsessive accuracy.

Some people may be more interested in the criminals whom Sheldon helps convict. I understand this. Readers have always craved an entrée into the world of the mad, bad and dangerous. And writers, from today's *Underbelly* scriptwriters back to the pious Christian seventeenth-century poet, John Milton, who made Satan the hero of his epic poem *Paradise Lost*, have always obliged them.

I also have my moments of wavering. I fight envy twinges when I share panels with writers who interview criminals or when I think of American true crime writer, Ann Rule, whose life as an author with an inside track on psychopaths began when she started on a book about a then unsolved series of murders of young women. Within a short time police had a promising suspect. Then Rule realised she *knew* him. They'd worked side by side a few years earlier on the suicide hotline at the Seattle Crisis Clinic.

I have good reasons for pitching my writing tent in the realm of the goody-goodies and document-ing the work of real-life forensic scientists and police officers. For a start, I love the topic. So much so that, between 1998 and 2009, I convinced various *Sunday Age* features editors to let me write dozens of 'real' stories about forensic science—solved crimes: articles that would debunk *CSI*-style misinformation and give readers the truth. Not that I'm knocking *CSI*. It was the fictional precursors of this program, which only began in 2000, that sparked my interest in forensic fact.

From the mid-1990s I was reading Patricia Cornwell novels and watching British forensic pathology dramas such as *Silent Witness* and *McCallum*. Listening to the crackle of the telepathologists' heavy plastic aprons as they paused, mid-dissection, to gossip about their love lives, I asked the standard fiction fan question: 'What is it really like?'

A few phone calls later I was on my way to witnessing my first post-mortem examination, wondering whether or not to eat breakfast beforehand. I spent three days at the Victorian Institute of Forensic Medicine (VIFM) and produced a 4000-word feature, which appeared in the *Sunday Age* in April 1998. In 2001 I profiled the VIFM's Dr David Wells. Formerly known as the 'police surgeon', he examines wounds on living victims, rather than dead 'silent witnesses'.

My curiosity extended to those forensic investiga-tors who deal with inanimate physical evidence. This, too, was sparked by fiction: namely the early 1990s ABC drama *Phoenix*, loosely based on the investigation of the 1986 bombing of Melbourne's Russell Street police headquarters. There were scenes in which forensic investigators reassembled the fatal bomb, one component of which was a piece of wood, possibly sawn from a fence. Police raided a suspect's home in search of a fence post with a chunk missing.

Via the Victoria Police media office, I contacted the Victoria Police Forensic Services Centre, based in the outer Melbourne suburb of Macleod. I told them I was hoping for a 'fence post'-style case to open with. I wanted to tell readers about the work of real-life crime scene investigators, but I needed a '*CSI* moment' to pull them in before I explained that real life wasn't like that.

Police media 'gave' me fire and bomb blast examiner George Xydias, whose work helped convict a man of the murder of his own child and the attempted murder of his wife. Xydias was able to show that an 'accidental' fatal fire, supposedly caused by a bedside aromatherapy burner falling into a box of tissues, had been a cold-blooded arson-murder. First, his experiments showed that mere tissues and a flame would not start a fire of such intensity. Second, that a fire of similar strength and speed could be replicated with the additional use of ether.

In 2003, after my article on Xydias appeared in the *Sunday Age*, a Pan Macmillan editor rang and suggested I write a book featuring a collection of such cases. At the time I would have described myself as a journalist and fledgling novelist. My first novel, *Unnatural Order*, had been published in 1995 and I had written a second but set it aside because it needed more work. I was also five chapters into a crime novel with a plan written out and an agent making encouraging noises.

One piece of writing advice I have always cherished (applicable to both fiction and nonfiction) is this: 'Try to do something a bit different from what everybody else is doing.' This maxim governed my start as a newspaper feature writer in Hong Kong, where I took a job in a 'girlie' bar, to write about what it's really like to go to work in an evening dress, chatting up men so they'd buy scandalously overpriced drinks that paid my wages. Most men in Hong Kong were fascinated by such places—and no woman had yet gone in undercover to write about one. The *Hong Kong Standard* ran my piece and I quit teaching.

I asked the same question of myself when I sat down to write a crime novel. 'Is it any different?' Sadly, it wasn't. However, the idea of writing a nonfiction book based on how forensic science was being used to solve crimes was something new that no other writer in Australia had done. So I ditched my 'novelist' identity to enter the world of true crime.

I told myself the transition would be easy. I was a journalist, wasn't I? I already had a title in mind: *Written on the Skin*. It had come to me when I described

Dr David Wells in the *Sunday Age* as 'a fluent reader of the ghastly language that fists and weapons write on human bodies'. The metaphor of 'reading' could also summarise each expert's relationship with the evidence he or she is called upon to interpret: data that is a foreign language to lay eyes and ears.

And how hard would it be to find cases covering all the forensic specialties? I could just ask the experts. I already knew some of them who could nominate colleagues in different areas. Of course the process wasn't that easy. First, I couldn't just rely on the scientists for information about the cases they had worked on. Contrary to the impression given by TV drama, forensic scientists are not part of a close-knit investigative team, living and breathing each case until it is solved. They work on many cases at once— and often will know only their aspect of each one. To fill out the whole story, I read trial transcripts and judgments, as well as the scientists' own reports, chased down inquest files and newspaper court reports and interviewed police and lawyers. In one case, I only discovered the existence of a groundbreaking covert DNA-gathering exercise when I unearthed a paper about it on the Internet. Names had been redacted, but I recognised the details of a case.

I often found myself reinterviewing scientists because research had thrown up topics they hadn't thought to mention. Sometimes court documents confirmed that, just like other human beings, police and scientists some-times conflate memories of different episodes.

Learning from this experience, I decided to research my second book, *Cold Case Files: Past crimes solved by new forensic science*, in the reverse order. I found the cases first and did the primary research before approaching scientists and detectives. By then I knew what I needed to know, not what they thought I'd want to know.

The process of writing also taught me that the border between the worlds of crime fiction and true crime is even more porous than we imagine. By using standard, fiction-writing techniques to recount real-life cases, I was making choices about narrative point of view and where in the story timeline to start. (Answer: whatever makes the most arresting opening.) I had to be conscious of maintaining narrative pace and creating suspense. Yes, the crime had been solved, but why not allow the reader to spend time wondering how? Maybe even let them piece the clues together?

Like any fiction writer I would need to provide telling physical details about the investigator, the perpetrator, the location and the weather on the day, only in this case, I couldn't make up these details—I had to research them.

Selecting this material is governed by many of the same criteria that govern crime fiction writers. We both aim to entertain readers. We tell stories. We introduce clues. However, most real-life murders are bereft of the interesting motives found in fiction. Forget 'hearts full of passion, jealousy and hate', to quote the song 'As Time

Goes By'. Too many true crime stories are banal and sad, or so bizarre and dysfunctional as to appear entirely unbelievable. Even more disappointing, most forensic work is done to *confirm* what police already know. Goodbye suspense.

I couldn't merely collect true stories. I had to find transgressions that most resembled the material of crime fiction. Real life does throw up such narratives, but you have to look hard.

I had wanted to begin *Written on the Skin* with one of VIFM deputy director Dr David Ranson's first cases: the identification of a decomposing headless body found in a northern Victorian mineshaft in 1988. The scientist had done extraordinary work, first identifying the remains as male and then using infra-red photography to show that discoloured areas on the victim's skin were not just random marks but the traces of highly idiosyncratic tattoos that could be used to identify him. Sadly, it being real life, all this wonderful work was only done to back up what police already knew. The dopey killers had cut off their victim's head so he couldn't be identified, but had left his dole papers in his back pocket. The cops were knocking on their door before Dr Ranson had put on his mortuary scrubs. This wasn't true *CSI*, it was *Dumb and Dumber*. So I cut it from the manuscript.

All good crime novelists nail the fine details of forensics, ballistics and police procedure, but my main reason for staying in the realm of forensic true crime is that I feel compelled to document the arduousness, the detail and the occasional apparent futility of the daily work of forensic and police investigators. They are often unsung heroes and their work, although fascinating, can be mind-numbingly tedious. Crime fiction dare not acknowledge this, for fear of killing its readers with boredom.

The fiction imperatives of plot and narrative tension demand some big lies. Forget the reality of 'clear-up rates', hung juries and failed prosecutions, fiction readers demand that crimes be solved, justice served and order restored. An unsolved crime is a fact of life for a real-life detective. In fiction, it's a shock.

Fictional detectives tend to be, and *need* to be, luckier than their real-life counterparts. The conventions of plot require that the investigation move forward quickly. There can be red herrings and blind corners, but the momentum builds like a snowball rolling down a slope. In real life, detectives can be starved of good leads. They set up information caravans at crime scenes, reinterview witnesses and plough through dozens of useless-looking tip-offs from the public.

In a crime novel the list of suspects tends to be improbably short, to avoid reader confusion. Three is a good number, but six is the maximum. The 1993 hunt for one of Melbourne's more notorious serial rapists generated 177 suspects, all ranked in order of apparent priority on the squad's whiteboard. When six-year-old

Sheree Beasley was abducted and murdered on Victoria's Mornington Peninsula in 1991, the list of suspects exceeded 250.

In the alternative fictional universe, forensic tests are produced quickly and solve the crime. Real-life invest-igations often move at a glacial pace—usually for banal reasons, such as rostered days off or a ban on overtime.

Call me a pedant, but I like readers to know all the above. I want them to understand that *real* forensic practitioners live a lab-bound existence, leavened by the occasional visit to a crime scene, and the eventual appearance in court. I want readers to know that some detectives spend years on a case and still never get a result—a sad truth made clear by *Baltimore Sun* reporter and creator of *The Wire*, David Simon, in his splendid nonfiction epic, *Homicide: A year on the killing streets*.

Most of all, I want readers to know that it is only on the rare, good days that the practice of crime invest-igation is worth comparing to the comforting thread of Ariadne, which she gave to Theseus so that he could unwind it through the labyrinth, kill the Minotaur and find his way out again. On most occasions the more appropriate mythical reference is to Sisyphus, whose eternal punishment was to keep rolling a huge boulder up a hill, only to have it tumble down again.

I wish to honour the heroism of investigators who get up every morning hoping to be Theseus, but can live with the reality of being Sisyphus.

MY RULES

1. Get to your desk by nine on weekdays, and don't leave until five, or until you have written 1500 words.

Ten a.m. to 6 p.m. is a permissible alternative.

2. 'Writer's block' is an affectation.

You may be struggling to find the right opening for a story or chapter. After decades of journalism, I know the sky will fall in if I don't have the 'lead par' right, so I just keep at it. The sensible alternative is to leave it and move forward in the narrative to a section that will slot in later. If you must, take a short break. A walk down the street for coffee, a short lunch, exercise. The solution will drop into your head as you walk back.

3. When a draft is close to ready, read it aloud to yourself so you know the rhythm is right.

4. Re-read your work with an eye to cutting unnecessary words (read crime writer and former champion newspaper subeditor Peter Temple for inspiration).

I note that Elmore Leonard's famous 'mortal sin' quote about excising adverbs applied to their use as a qualifier for 'said' or (horrors!) synonyms. Only use an adverb if you can't find an alternative.

5. Beware of 'dangling modifiers'—too many copyeditors don't pick them up.

The dreaded DM is a misplaced opening phrase which appears to qualify the noun immediately after it. 'Running down the street, her handbag fell in a muddy puddle.' The handbag was not doing the running. Rewrite.

6. Keep your writing muscular.

Let the verbs do as much work as possible.

7. Be conscious of the 'power' spots in sentences: the first words, the last words.

Examine what you put there.

8. Too much research is the right amount.

The details you know but held back, to keep the pace moving, are the powerful nine-tenths of the iceberg.

9. If you can find the willpower to disable your Internet while writing, do so.

And change your phone settings. Only check your email twice a day. Yes, you will need to Google to check the spelling of the contents of gun residue. Leave a space and do all that checking at the end of the working day.

10. Don't just rely on your publisher's proofreader.

Make four copies of your final edited manuscript and hand them out to the kind of friends you've heard comment on mistakes in already published books. Read it yourself twice, including once aloud (that is the only way you will pick up a mistake such as 'women' instead of 'woman').

FIVE MUST-READS

1. Homicide: A year on the killing streets by David Simon

2. The Tall Man: Death and life on Palm Island by Chloe Hooper

3. Wyatt by Garry Disher

4. Tete-a-tete: Simone de Beauvoir and Jean-Paul Sartre by Hazel Rowley

5. Fear and Loathing in Las Vegas by Hunter S. Thompson

Liz Porter is a journalist who began her career in Hong Kong and then worked in Sydney, London and Stuttgart before returning to her hometown of Melbourne, where she is a regular contributor to the Age and the Sunday Age. She has won awards for her writing on legal issues and her book, Written on the Skin, was joint winner of the 2007 Ned Kelly Award for Best True Crime Book.

I'M WRITING A CRIME NOVEL

by Garry Disher

I'm writing a crime novel.

Good on you. What kind?

What do you mean, what kind?

Courtroom drama, whodunit, private-eye story, forensic invest-igation, missing-person case, police procedural, caper novel . . . ?

Well, a murder mystery obviously.

Why is it obvious? It could be a mystery about arson, corruption, sexual assault, blackmail, theft, confidence trickery, gangland strife, drug dealing, arms dealing, extortion, kidnap, embezzlement . . .

There *has* to be a murder!

Not necessarily. Not every crime novel begins with a body. The murder could occur at the end as fallout from something deeper and darker. What's the motive for your murder?

Well, hate.

Or revenge, jealousy, greed, concealment, lust, the need for a pre-emptive strike . . . Who's your main character?

A detective.

Police detective, private eye, amateur detective, accidental hero, investigative journalist, lawyer, mediaeval monk, Roman centurion, 1920s flapper, Oxford-educated English aristo-crat . . . ?

Police detective.

Where's it set?

Well, urban.

Melbourne? Sydney? LA?

Does it matter? Murder is universal.

Fair enough. Is it in the style of writers you admire?

Mate, I don't *read* the stuff. Guys like James Patterson make millions a year, that's all I need to know.

This is only a slight exaggeration of the conversations I sometimes find myself having, backed into a corner at a festival venue, library nook or classroom. And each time it confirms to me that crime fiction is generally under-valued and misunderstood.

Yet it is infinitely rewarding. For a start, we get a story. This might sound self-evident, but consider those 'literary' novels you read sometimes, full of beautiful prose, extraordinary characters and absorbing themes— *but in which nothing happens.* People need stories, and the narrative drive of crime fiction is a great part of its appeal.

Not that story alone can suffice. If we don't care about the characters, then the most cunning and unexpected twists, turns, reversals and revelations ever imagined will fall flat. Character is the central element of storytelling, and readers enjoy travelling with the heroes (and the anti-heroes), sharing their triumphs and setbacks.

This wasn't always true of crime fiction. The 'golden age' novels of Agatha Christie and others concentrated on the puzzle at the expense of character. Readers gained little insight into Miss Marple's inner or private life other than a sense of a keen intellect at work. The mid-twentieth-century American private-eye novels were no better, with their bourbon-drinking, wisecracking, hired-by-blondes-with-big-breasts investigators. Unknowable men. Unreachable.

Then the genre renewed itself. Writers like Sara Paretsky and Sue Grafton entered the field, giving us heroes we could relate to, with their messy love lives, mistakes, reluctance to get hit over the head, empty fridges, moral indecisiveness and, most importantly, a social context of lovers, parents, friends, neighbours and siblings. They made their characters real to us.

Crucially, however, they are *not* us. They go where we fear to tread—which is why we admire them so much. Where we are hedged in by doubts and scruples, they act. We wouldn't dream of telling the boss to get stuffed or expect the cavalry to ride up at the last moment. They have no such reservations.

There are many other virtues. Crime fiction is often topical, a barometer of prevailing social tensions, telling us about the world we live in, exploring the effects on individuals, families and communities of institutional corruption, fraud, the drugs trade, racism, poverty, misogyny, homophobia and domestic violence.

Crime fiction appeals to our senses. Good writing makes 'pictures in the head', and crime writers are adept at helping readers taste the acrid stake-out coffee, smell the toxins, hear the footsteps in the alleyway, touch the spilt blood, see the flicker in the killer's eyes.

There are vicarious pleasures. A manhunt might have us on the edges of our seats, the technical know-how may fascinate (to a degree: who cares if a certain 9mm automatic has a ten- or a twelve-cartridge clip?), and it can be heart-quickening to see the painstaking stages of an investigation begin to arrive at the truth (readers are quick to dismiss the hero who does no work but relies on luck, friends and flashes of inspiration).

We like to feel the screws tighten—suspense and tension, in other words. Any story that starts with a question generates immediate suspense. A love story might ask, 'Will the lovers get together at the end?' and a crime story might ask, 'Who is the killer?' or 'Will she get away with it?' But, once created, the suspense needs to be sustained, the tension needs to mount, and to achieve it a crime novelist will use certain tricks of the trade (these I am about to reveal—after which I will have to kill you).

Charles Dickens said it best: 'Make 'em laugh, make 'em cry, make 'em *wait*.'

Readers crave an answer to the unspoken question driving a story, but skilled writers don't satisfy that craving, or not immediately, or not totally, or not in the form expected or desired by readers. They use delaying and withholding tactics, give partial or doubtful outcomes, reveal hidden secrets only at the end. Knowing the importance of the puzzle element, they don't spell things out, but encourage readers to read actively, negotiating with the information and speculating about motives and possible outcomes.

At the same time, writers will subvert expectations, get readers to concentrate on the wrong issue or character, and, just when the reader—and the hero—is standing comfortably, pull the rug out from beneath them.

Tricks—crime writers revel in them, as long as they're not cheap or tacked on merely to shock or entertain, or a means of getting the hero over a brick wall ('With a mighty bound, he was free . . .').

Finally, crime fiction appeals to deep but contradictory impulses in us all: to commit the perfect crime and to make things right. I'd be a master criminal if I had the nerve: I'd rob a bank, I'd kill those who've done me wrong. Yet I'd also be a lawman if I had the nerve. I would restore order and mete out justice in a world governed by chance, misfortune, and the actions of the vicious, the undeserving and the dishonest.

Safe behind their desks, crime writers do have the nerve. They know their just and fearless sides, just as they know their darker sides. The great themes of literature are love, hate, honour, greed and betrayal, and any one of them may lie behind a crime.

Okay, okay, you know all that . . . What you'd like is advice on getting started.

You won't get far if you're not curious, single-minded and able to stand back and take the long view—able, quoting Graham Greene, to write with a chip of ice in your heart. Storytellers are alert to the plot potential in everything they see, hear and feel, everything that catches their attention—a dream, a newspaper clipping, a *what if?* thought, a woman glimpsed slapping a man's face at a tram stop, a friend's scary experience, a personal heartache, a teenager overheard saying, 'Everything went wrong when Grandma came to live with us.'

From such random beginnings, a writer will interrogate the idea, to see if a story or a character will emerge. Like any person, they might be curious to know what really went wrong when Grandma came to stay, but as Edward Albee said, 'Fiction is fact, distorted into truth', and a writer will invent an explanation by asking: 'Why did Grandma come to stay?'

'What happens next?' 'What if she hadn't come?' 'What if she dies?' 'Is she a divisive or a cohesive presence?' 'Is she the maternal or the paternal grandmother?' 'What if she's very rich?' 'What if she's found dead one morning?'

Gradually characters, incidents and plot strands take shape. Give it time. I have sat on some ideas for years, knowing they were incomplete, immature or in want of an unlocking idea. I've also spent months writing a novel before realising I'd overreached and was padding out a perfectly fine short story. (My pet hate is the 'big book bloat' of some American crime novels.)

My first Challis and Destry novel, *The Dragon Man*, developed from a mix of actual events, personal experiences and speculation. Soon after moving to the Mornington Peninsula I began thinking about writing a series of police procedurals set in Melbourne, where I'd lived for twenty years. But one day I entered a nearby small-town milk bar and overheard the shopkeeper and her customers discussing the abduction, rape and murder of three young women near Frankston, an outer suburb at the head of the peninsula. There was fear in their voices: they were the parents of teenage daughters who now couldn't walk along the street or catch a bus unchaperoned. Here was a small regional community under siege to a serial murderer, and the novelist in me saw a more fertile setting for a series of police procedurals than yet another big city. And so it has proved to be: the Peninsula novels are as much about a setting and a way of life as crime and detection.

Then while writing the first novel, loosely based on the Frankston murders, I had two slightly troubling experiences that I reworked fictionally, bringing some much-needed texture to the story. I live on a quiet back road, and one night my letterbox was set alight. My neighbours' boxes were similarly vandalised. First reaction: householder outrage. Second reaction: novelistic curiosity. What manner of person set fire to my letterbox? Why? Was he or she alone? I began to see two young men in my mind's eye, drunk, high, idle, viciously bored. *And what if one of them learns that lighting fires gives him a particular thrill . . . ?*

The other incident was my fault: I gave the finger to a driver who'd cut me off in his massive 4WD. Such men and women are monarchs of the road and this one followed me home and staked out the end of my driveway, engine throbbing, for some time. For weeks afterwards I feared he might come back.

At the same time I was also wondering, *What if I'd led him to someone else's house before making my way home after he'd gone?* I know, shameful, but it gave me a great plot twist.

Some crime novelists tell you they don't plan, but follow where their noses or their characters take them. Others do plan, sometimes in minute detail. There is no right or wrong way. James Ellroy wrote a 211-page outline before embarking on *LA Confidential*; James Lee Burke never sees more than two pages around the corner and revises as he goes along; Agatha Christie would do domestic chores until the whole story was in her head before sitting down to write; Tony Hillerman often didn't know the identity or motive of the culprit until the last chapter; P.D. James plans for eighteen months and writes for eighteen months.

I'm a planner. Sean O'Faolain argued that three elements are necessary at the start: a character, a situation and a promise; if these aren't present then I don't get very far. With a crime and a criminal in mind, and a feeling for their potential, I'll spend weeks, sometimes months, dreaming my way deeper into the circumstances of the crime and why it occurred and who it affects and how it will be investigated, all the while scribbling observations, speculations and questions onto the backs of my old manuscripts, using a blue-ink ballpoint pen (creativity would fly out the window if I used black).

As the general shape emerges, I take the four main stages—set-up, complications, a groping towards the truth, the truth revealed—into chapters. The chapters are mini stories: they involve characters, a setting and a mood, and necessarily advance the story in some way rather than mark time, repeat what's already known or indulge some fine writing.

At the same time, I'll test the plan: Would he do that, given the type of person he is? If she's a midwife, how did she learn how to hack into the Pentagon? What would happen if he did X instead of Y? What if the uncle was murdered instead of the aunt? Is it better to introduce her before or after the arrest? Do I need the neighbour?

These questions also help me finetune the characters' movements in time and place. I learned the importance of this when the editor of *The Dragon Man* pointed out that, logically, my hero had received a letter on a Sunday, that no-one can leave Melbourne at peak hour on a Friday and reach Mornington an hour later, and if Tuesday is publication day for a weekly newspaper, it can't cover a breaking story until the following Tuesday.

At last the whole book is mapped out. It describes a perfect, shimmering path through strange territory, and all I have to do is follow it . . . unless my instincts tell me otherwise.

I've learned to listen to the needling voice. I'd framed my (non-crime) novel, *The Stencil Man*, about a German immigrant interned as a security risk during the Second World War, as a prison novel, but then, several months into the writing, I heard a voice say: *Martin's going to escape.* I stopped writing in order to listen (long walks helped). Initially, I conceived of *The Stencil Man* as a novel about a character under strain in an enclosed setting, not a thriller, and needed to know if Martin's escape was believable and inevitable rather than a cheap attempt to generate plot thrills. Tied up in this question was another: Would so mild a man take this action? Causation is everything in fiction, however deeply buried.

For the first and only time, I was led by one of my characters. Martin let me know what drove him, and I helped him to escape—which meant I had to recast the first two-thirds of the novel to lay the groundwork for it.

Character is more important than plot. In fact, characters are plotting aids. It's not enough for us to know them by their personality traits: they must also *act* and their actions must have consequences. The ideal is a balance of plot and character interest, with plot events growing out of the characters, not grafted onto them.

How does this apply to series characters? If my Challis and Destry novels told the same story over and over again, and the characters' relationship dynamics never altered, interest would soon pall—for writer and reader. And so by the later novels the young constable in the first novel is a trainee detective, a troubled marriage has ended, Sergeant Destry has equal billing with Inspector Challis, and I'm about to jettison one of the minor characters.

What about research? Some American crime writers spend pages acknowledging the help and advice of law enforcement types, coroners, lawyers, forensic scientists, armourers. I'm a little lazy.

Obviously I strive for accuracy and authenticity when I describe a weapon, a crime scene, an autopsy— we've all had letters along the lines of, 'Wyatt couldn't have wheeled that Chubb safe out of the building because it would have been cemented into the floor'— but I think readers' eyes glaze over if there's too much technical detail. I'm more interested in technical *failure* than method—cross-contamination in the forensic lab because the lab technician wore the same pair of gloves all day, for example. I have used the police as a research source from time to time, finding them to be friendly, approachable and pleased that someone's taking an interest in their work, not maligning them. Otherwise I'll use the Internet and my local library, or contact specialists (a gun shop owner once told me—by phone, having never met me—that it's easy to 'rebirth' a handgun by replacing the barrel). And I've learned not to trust other writers. In one of Robert B. Parker's novels a gunman collects the shells ejected by his *revolver*.

Could my writing habits help *you* write a novel?

I produce one novel a year, writing six mornings a week whether I feel like it or not. While welcoming inspiration, I don't wait for it. Inspiration is a sentence scribbled on a scrap of paper, after all: I still need to write the thousands of sentences that flesh it out. Writing unlocks the mind, thumb-twiddling does not.

If only it would get easier. The more I know, the more I realise I don't know, and the more I want to push at my boundaries. Invariably, things go wrong: I might overreach, discover I'm writing two novels and need to split the work, or rethink the identity of the killer at the page-proof stage (as happened with *Snapshot*), or realise, one year and 40 000 words later, that I need to start again (call me a slow learner . . .).

MY RULES

I stand by these rules of writing:

1. **It's not enough to talk and think about writing: write.**

2. **Be alert to the fictional potential in everything in and around you.**

3. **Write every day rather than a splurge every few weeks.**

4. **If you're not serious about your story, your readers won't be either.**

5. **Read: many aspiring writers don't.**

6. **Take risks—so long as they're not cheap effects but true to the material.**

7. **Become part of the community of writers in some way:**
   join a writers' centre, a book club or a creative-writing group; talk to knowledgeable booksellers and librarians; read book reviews; enrol in a writing course.

8. **Don't let how-to books, writing courses and other authors make you anxious or cause you to second-guess what works for you.**

9. **Over-confidence is as crippling as under-confidence.**

10. **Don't be under the misapprehension that everything you write must be new, original or different from what's been published before.**

   Storytellers tell the same stories over and over again. In fact, it's been said that there are only seven plots:

Crime and punishment

The worm turns

The eternal triangle

The quest

Revenge

Slaying the dragon

Boy meets girl.

FIVE MUST-READS

1. **The entire series of Maj Sjöwall and Per Wahlöö's Inspector Beck novels**

2. **The Pied Piper** by Ridley Pearson

3. **LaBrava** by Elmore Leonard

4. **Miami Blues** by Charles Willeford

5. **The Broken Shore** by Peter Temple

Garry Disher *is one of Australia's most successful authors, having published more than 40 books in a range of genres. Best known for his two crime series, Wyatt and the Challis and Destry novels, which are growing in popularity in Australia, Europe and the United States, Garry has twice won Best Crime Novel in the Ned Kelly Awards.*

NED KELLY DIARY

by Malla Nunn

Prelude

I accepted the invitation to contribute to this book
of writerly wisdom because Michael Robotham was
cunning enough to use the words 'leading crime writers'
in the invitation, so I felt compelled to say yes. I'm still
not sure how much wisdom, if any, I can possibly offer
because I write instinctively and don't plot my novels
in advance. Instead, I hope my characters will guide
me through to the end and that the journey will be
memorable for readers. This 'blind trust' approach has
served me well, so I've used it again with this essay,
patching together my daily thoughts on writing. You
can find them below in the same rough order as they
came to me.

In the beginning

I grew up in rural Swaziland, a former British protectorate in Southern Africa. Books were a luxury. Nursing, teaching and marriage were acceptable career options for females. They were good choices with job security and long-service leave. If only I'd listened.

While books other than the Bible were hard to find, there was a strong oral tradition in our isolated community. People told stories. Aunties exchanged tales. Uncles embellished on that time the fat Dutch policeman pulled them over at the border and demanded ID papers. What a buffoon, with his gun and inferior English. Stories had value. They informed and entertained. Growing up, I was caught up in the enjoyment of hearing the details and imagining the scene, living vicariously through the teller. The best stuff was whispered among the adults: the cousin up on murder charges, that mad doctor in Manzini who groped Mrs Brown's breasts, the niece who 'had to get married'.

We were good Christians, but clearly there was this other, darker place under the churchy surface. That's the world that caught my imagination. Listening to impossible tales and watching the rare movies that made it down to our end of the country brought a kind of magic into my small world. By osmosis, the desire to create became part of my DNA. Yet it didn't even cross my mind that there were people in the world who made up stories for a living. This knowledge came much later. However the seed for becoming a crime writer was planted. I was hooked.

Getting out of my own way

Long before I started writing, I was in awe of famous crime writers, dazzled by Walter Mosley's smooth ghetto dialogue, James Lee Burke's smoking atmosphere, Arthur Upfield's love of the land and Minette Walters' perverted English countryside. Compete with them? Who was I kidding? I didn't have the talent, the devious twists of mind that every crime writer needs to shine in a crowded genre market. By comparing myself to my favourite established authors, I prevented myself for years from beginning a novel of my own.

What I know now is this: the quickest way out of the mental ghetto of negative comparison is to write. Write through the anxiety. Some days the words on the page will be good, and some days utter rubbish. Write anyway. Every story is a leap of faith. Trust your story enough to finish it. The publishing world and the reading public already have books by these famous writers. What the publishers and readers don't have, yet, is a book by *you*.

Only you can write like you. Your style is unique. Your stories come from your own personal well and that is a very specific place with its own magic. Dig deep and write. That's all.

That's a great idea

Ideas won't keep. Something must be done about them.
Alfred North Whitehead

People ask, 'Where do you get your ideas?' The answer is, 'From everywhere.' Crime writers are lucky. The world has yet to run out of criminals or victims. Story ideas are broadcast, published, gossiped about and discussed every single day. Crime is international and its impact is universal. Keep your ears and eyes open.

Often, ideas come hand-delivered. The local community paper is thrown onto my front lawn once a week. There's a small section, a quarter of a page, listing court appearances and police charges. This section is gold. Not on a 'this is my next story' level, but in a more subtle way. It seems that no matter how stable a society, people continue to break the law. Crime rates have dropped, but on any given week the police continue to lay charges. The usual suspects make the top four list of crimes: physical assault, fraud, theft and driving under the influence.

Some weeks there are more complex cases; a Chinese businessman murdered by his male Ghanaian lover; a cache of partially assembled assault rifles found in the garage of an ordinary double-brick house on a very ordinary street; the con woman who preyed on the elderly by offering to 'bless' a piece of jewellery in return for using the phone. And so it goes, all over the planet.

The likelihood of my using any of the above stories or characters as they appear is slim. I might. There's no copyright on individual crimes and writers are, by their very nature, thieves. Reading the local crime report puts me in the right frame of mind. I'm often left wondering, 'Why?' Why was this particular crime committed and was there a way to avoid it? The local paper is an invitation to exercise my imagination. Ten minutes once a week over a cup of tea I get to read about greed and desire, ponder their meaning and find explanations for those two things. It's 'work', and it gives me a delicious voyeuristic pleasure.

Coming up with an answer to the question of 'why' is fundamentally what crime fiction is all about. Psychiatry has labels for extreme human behaviour. Yet rarely am I satisfied with a simple, 'She killed her three children because she was clinically depressed,' or 'He stabbed his girlfriend in a jealous rage.' I long to know more, in graphic detail. How did things get so bad?

Ideas are constant. They come in a variety of shapes and guises. Find them where you can. My books are set in 1950s South Africa and I source character details from photography books from that era. People looked and dressed differently then. Fedora hats, ironed sundresses, gloves and two-tone shoes; photographs open a window into a past world. There's a stack of black-and-white images on my desk for reference, but my father is also a living reference book. I ask him about the food he ate and the music he listened to. We talk. He tells me stories, many of which end up having no bearing on the book I'm writing, but I love hearing them just the same. I read novels written during the time period and watch films with femmes fatales and tough men in suits. None of this feels like work. In a way I'm playing, feeding my mind.

Making a physical space

It's good to have a 'room of one's own', but if that's not possible then make a nook, find a corner, dig a hole in which you can partially shelter from the noise of everyday life. Stephen King wrote *Carrie* in the laundry room of an apartment building. Ray Bradbury took himself to the public library and fed coins into a 'dime-at-a-time' typewriter. Nine days and $9.80 in dimes later came the short story, 'The Fireman', which later transformed into *Fahrenheit 451*. A friend wrote a fine novel on a small desk in the corner of her bedroom. My first book, *A Beautiful Place to Die*, was written a few pages at a time on the kitchen table when the house was empty.

Stephen King suggests a room with a door that can be closed. Great idea. Three novels later, I've upgraded to a desk in the corner of the kitchen. Work with what you have. If all endeavours fail, run away from home. Go on a writer's retreat. Anyone with a weekender or a holiday house should go to the top of your 'be-nice-to-this-person' list. Before my first week-long retreat to a friend's mother's house on the central coast, I confided to another pal that leaving the family seemed selfish. He replied, 'It is. But what's wrong with that?' So I went and experienced first hand the supremely selfish pleasure of having nothing else to do but write.

Building a room for your imaginary friends

Clearing a physical space is important, but accessing a mental space for your stories to grow and flourish is vital. Your characters are not physically manifested. They cannot defend themselves. You must defend them. Treat your characters as if they were real. Talk to them daily. Listen to them. Invite them to sit a while. Take them to an art gallery to enjoy an exhibition. They are important. Ignore them and they will, like neglected children, wander off and find new homes. One day you might encounter them again, living in a book by another author.

The mental space you build to shelter your characters should be a fort with strong walls and buckets of burning tar to repel attacks by the real world. On a practical level, this means leaving the laundry to pile up for a few days (nobody ever died of a stained shirt) or opening a can of soup for dinner two nights in a row. Yes, I know this sounds very domestic and dull, but none of us is James Bond. When Raymond Carver was asked, 'What are your greatest influences?' He replied,

'My children. Without them I would have written so much more.'

Single, married, divorced or in a blended family, it is a struggle to clear a space in which to feed and nourish stories. And that's the trick: balancing the demands of the real world against the fictional one. Both are real. Both require energy.

Tools of the trade

You don't need much: an idea, a piece of paper and a pen, or a laptop with a place to plug it in. A decent vocabulary and a thesaurus will help. Writing is a democratic art. We all begin equally: with a blank page and a desire to fill it. There is no one right way to make the jump from idea to the written word. If there were, writer's block wouldn't exist and deadlines would be easy to make. Different writers have individual ways of breaking into a book. Ian McEwan says that he 'drifts' into his novels. I make longhand notes on characters, scenes and themes, in no particular order. This stage is wonderful. Nothing is 'wrong' or 'right'. It's play. I read over the notes later and ask questions: Did the victim die in bed or is there a detail that I'm missing? Who's lying and why?

These are pretty much the same questions my main character, Detective Sergeant Emanuel Cooper, might ask when he arrives on scene. He doesn't know in advance what led to the crime or why flowers have been scattered across the body. We're both searching for answers. We investigate together. This is writing without the safety net of a beat-by-beat plot line under the story. Accidents happen and wrong turns are taken. Characters drop out and new ones appear. It's frustrating but also exhilarating when the unexpected happens. The satisfying 'click' when a piece of the crime puzzle fits into place is the reason I sit at a desk day after day, tapping away at the keys of my laptop.

In his book *On Writing*, Stephen King suggests that writers don't actually construct, they discover. Like explorers or anthropologists, we excavate the bones of the story one at a time. When that broken leg or purse of gold is uncovered, it's a surprise and it's thrilling. In the moment when a character reveals a secret or tells me a fact that I didn't know, I'm discovering the story, bringing it to light from a place where it already existed, waiting for me to find it.

Rationally I understand that I'm in control. The stories, the characters, the placement of clues need thought and consideration. That's why I walk to the park and to the shops to pick up that forgotten bunch of coriander. I keep notebooks, which are often hard to decipher when I'm done writing the book. Some mornings I sit for a moment to watch the bees. I am planning in an unforced way, letting my mind pick through the debris for the vein of gold.

This slightly crunch-granola, spirit-catcher method will not suit everyone. There is no one right way to break into a story. I have my freewheeling approach. Other writers plot every story beat and line of dialogue in advance. Before the beginning of a new book my husband says, 'You are going to plan this one, aren't you?' I say, 'Of course,' and then wander off to water the lettuce.

The modern age

How to resist the Internet? If you have an answer to this vexing question, let me know.

Research

Inspiration is more important than knowledge.
Albert Einstein

I'm with Albert. Details are important, but getting the story and the characters right are even more so. For the length of the first draft I let common sense be my guide. I use what I already know of 1950s South Africa—the bad roads, restrictive liquor laws, unreliable power supply and the rigid social order. What I don't know will keep until the second draft. Unless the exact colour of a police van in 1953 is central to the plot it can be added or changed later.

I then employ Terence, a former South African policeman, to read the manuscript for inaccuracies and to correct matters of procedure. He understands that crime books are not meant to mirror reality or replicate it. We established a key rule early: if he could prove that something in my story had never, ever happened in the history of South Africa, he was free to draw a red line through it. The ink in the red pen has since mostly dried up. We have, together, changed character names and finetuned character attitudes. Sometimes language is adjusted to reflect the times. Specific laws are clarified. Terence visits the police archive and digs through the records. He has my back.

While there is value in getting things right, research should never overwhelm character. This easily happens. If you've spent long hours collecting information and documenting, say, the inner workings of the tax office, the urge to use every tantalising detail is tempting. My researcher found out an interesting fact about prostitution laws in 1953 South Africa.[1] I tried three times, unsuccessfully, to insert this fact into the text, but just couldn't make it work so it had to go. Beware. 'Infodumping' is a leading cause of death for stories. Research must be woven seamlessly into the story.

A case in point: I'm a devotee of Philip Kerr's *Berlin Noir Trilogy* and of ex-policeman turned private eye Bernie Gunther. Kerr's control of time and place is masterful. Berlin in the 1940s comes alive. The cityscape is exact, with street names and famous landmarks throughout. Pre-war tensions simmer. Power shifts from the old guard to the resurgent National Socialist Party.

Kerr has obviously researched Berlin. Not once did I stop to consult an actual map of 1943 Berlin for cross-reference or wonder if that strudel shop on the corner really existed. I didn't need or want to check the facts. Bernie Gunther was my guide. He drank and fought through the seedy heart of the city. The books are well researched, but without Bernie they are history books: great for the archives and for tourists on a retro-tour of wartime Berlin.

You do need to get the facts right, but here's the thing: crime fiction readers don't read to acquire geographical, medical or historical knowledge. I certainly don't. I read crime fiction for the story, the atmosphere, for the thrill of the chase, for the drama. If these elements are missing, what's the point?

Research is the detailing on the car, not the car itself. It will make a vehicle more attractive but won't give it an engine or petrol.

Why crime?

My first attempt at a full-length novel was a romance. It turns out that romance is a common starting point for fledgling writers. I'd last read a romance in high school and asked myself, 'Boy meets Girl. How hard can it be?'

The rejection notes were polite. The last one, which I wish I'd kept to pin above my work desk, said that while the story was well written, 'prostitution and sexual dysfunction' had no place in a romance novel. That was twenty years ago.

As it turned out, I was well ahead of my time. The romance I'd written crossed genre lines. It was a crime novel dressed in a saucy frock with a satin bow. I had no idea. I hadn't taken the time to familiarise myself with the romance genre or learn the rules of romantic fiction.

A long way down the road, with a couple of short films on my CV and children in pre-school, came my first crime novel. I didn't consciously choose crime because I thought, 'A warm body and a smoking gun, how hard can it be?' I was a huge fan of the genre and read crime books for enjoyment. Strangely, my appetite for crime increased after having children. The local library stocked mysteries set in Victorian England, ancient Rome, modern-day London and the frozen Russian tundra. I worked through warm cosies and blood-splattered forensics and barely touched one per cent of the offerings.

The crime fiction canon is huge. Reading crime opened up a dark and dangerous world from which I'd emerge safe and in time for the evening news. Crime offered the quickest and widest window from my suburban house to the mean streets of every city and village on the planet.

The crime genre is generous. It's inclusive. It has no boundaries. It speaks to universal human fears. And in the best hands, helps soothe those fears. I felt, instinctively, there was a pew in this vast church marked especially for my South African detective and for me. I entered the genre without cynical intentions or expectations. I wrote what I loved to read.

I still do.

The door to crime fiction is open. The price of entry is a story. The only way to make this story is to write it. So, write.

Endnote

[1] The only province in South Africa where prostitution was a criminal activity in 1952 was the Transvaal.

FIVE MUST-READS

1. **The Bible:** *A great introduction to the big themes of good vs evil, human weakness and temptation.*

2. **Devil in a Blue Dress** *by Walter Mosley: Because it made me want to write crime fiction.*

3. **Cry the Beloved Country** *by Alan Paton: The human tragedy of the South African apartheid laws told with simple elegance.*

4. **Perfume** *by Patrick Süskind: A serial killer novel like no other.*

5. **Gilead** *by Marilynne Robinson: Beautifully observed meditation on the life of a small-town preacher.*

Malla Nunn was born in Swaziland in Southern Africa and moved to Australia in her early teens. An award-winning documentary maker, Malla is the author of three Emanuel Cooper novels set in 1950s South Africa, which have achieved critical acclaim around the world.

SCENES FROM A LIFE

by Kerry Greenwood

First scene

A child is sitting under a kitchen table, playing with her blocks. These are not neat plastic coloured blocks, but carpenter's off-cuts from her grandfather's workshop; irregular, curved and triangular—much more engrossing objects with which to build.

She is sickly, thin and needs to stay warm, and the kitchen is the only warm room in the house because it has a fire. Under the table she attracts no attention and the inhabitants forget that she is there. So they talk, over her head. Words flow over and around her like a soft tide: wharfie's talk, soldier's talk, memories, women's gynaecological agonies, gossip, jokes, recipes, snatches of song, music-hall jokes and hymns. She is three years old and absorbs this information like a sponge—odd words and hard words and peculiar concepts, which she doesn't understand but will remember and examine later. She will also horrify her mother by singing 'The Sexual Life of the Camel', which no-one can remember ever performing in her presence.

Second scene

The child is sitting on her mother's lap and they are reading her favourite book. She fiercely resists any attempt to introduce new literature. It is *Katie the Kitten*, a Little Golden Book, and her weary mother can recite every word. 'Katie the Kitten, a small tiger cat (turn page) is asleep in a hall (turn page) in a ball (turn page) in a hat.' And the child realises that the black marks on the page are words, and she can read them. And the world starts turning into printed words that can be read.

After that she reads everything. Cornflakes packets. Newspapers. Dictionaries. Aspirin bottles. The world is full of words.

Third scene

The child is holding her mother's hand outside a school gate. The gate is cyclone wire. She is five and thin and sick and she really wants to go home. Boys run and scream. One falls over on the pitiless asphalt and skins his knee. There is blood. All the child can see are knees and skirts. She bruises her nose on a shopping bag.

Then she spies a child just her height. She has beautiful

brown eyes, a basin haircut, and a purple velveteen dress with orange sky rockets even more unsightly than her own orange-stained yellow hand-me-down. The child puts out her hand. The other child takes hers. The other child says, '*Parakalo*'. The child realises that there are other languages in the world of words. She rejoices. And she has a friend. Now the world of words includes Greek, which provides the roots of so many English words.

Fourth scene

The child has measles. Although no longer feverish or delirious, her skin is pocked with hundreds of little, incredibly itchy sores. They are down her throat and in her hair and she is forbidden to scratch or she will be scarred. Worse, she is forbidden to read, because her eyes are very sensitive to light and will be damaged if she tries. Her window is shaded with a water-stained Holland blind.

Her mother visits as often as she can, but she has housework to do and another child to care for. Her grandmother sits and tells her fairytales, but she has had to go home. It is hours until dark.

The itching is intolerable without something else to think about. She rubs rather than scratches the sores in her hair. She is crazy with boredom. She is about to claw off those scabs and scar herself for life.

Then the water stain on the blind begins to turn into an island. *Treasure Island*. She has just finished the book.

The spot marked on Billy Bones' map is just beyond that beach. And all she needs to do is row the boat. She conjures the boat. And slips effortlessly into the story.

When the water stain vanishes with the coming of the darkness, it does not matter. Now she will never be bored again.

I wrote my first novel when I was sixteen. I was sitting in an old apricot tree in my parents' back garden. I had by that time three siblings and had discovered that none of them could climb.

That summer holiday seemed to stretch on forever, as they often do at that age. When I wasn't studying, I perched in the apricot tree keeping watch on the other children and writing a long, long fantasy called *The Magic Stone*, a pale and shonky imitation of *The Lord of the Rings*—a book I still love and read at least once a year. Aloud.

The Magic Stone was derived from Tolkien and from *Myths and Legends of Many Lands* (which was in the bookcase) and from Chaucer and from C.S. Lewis and Bob Dylan and—everything, really.

Writing novels is my secret vice (not so secret now; I have outed myself), in which I indulge with such pleasure that it verges on indecent. Those early efforts weren't read by anyone else (and no-one else will ever see *The Magic Stone*), but I cherished and nurtured those stories, hugging them close against the cold of the real world. They were—and are—my escape from loss and grief and illness and death. When the world didn't suit me, when I was miserable or upset, I wrote heart-rending tales of tragedy and broken hearts. When I was angry, I wrote bloody revenge fantasies.

The affable and charming Colin Wilson, whom I met at Melbourne Writers Festival some years ago, said that no writer has ever killed anyone. That's because we don't need to kill people, we can write them into a detective story and slay them in various entertaining ways. It's so much less messy than actually killing them and—I imagine—just as satisfying albeit without the karmic debt and the jail sentence.

I continued to write through school and into university, where I was studying Law, which was difficult, and English, which was fun, and such miscellaneous subjects as Art and Philosophy and History. In particular, I found the 1740 period in England fascinating and discovered that the Baillieu Library at the University of Melbourne had books about the city of St Albans in England, along with facsimiles of the original municipal records. I used these to research eight novels that featured a highwayman called Matthew Benjamin who operated outside St Albans in 1740.

Since I was writing to escape from the real world, I never wrote about the present, preferring the past and sometimes the future. The present was full of law exams and poverty. But the past, ah, there were feasts in the past.

I joined Melbourne University Choral Society (MUCS) and sang madrigals, ballads and folk songs at the *Three Drunken Maidens* for jugs of cider. It was more words, more ways of saying things. Ballads often start in the middle of the story. No introduction, no explanation, no scene setting. They are fairytales pared down to the bones.

> *My mother did me deadly spite*
> *For she sent thieves in the dark of the night*
> *Put my servants all to flight*
> *They robbed my bower, they slew my knight.*

This is a stanza from 'The Famous Flower of Serving-Men', a murder ballad. Nobody knows why her mother hates her so much that she orders her knight and her baby slaughtered, but the song ends with a very satisfying execution as the mother is burned at the stake. No detail is omitted.

> *For the fire took first upon her cheek*
> *And then it took all on her chin*
> *It spat and rang in her yellow hair*
> *And soon there was no life left in.*

This is just one of 305 songs in a collection known as the Child Ballads. There are five volumes, which were given to me by my parents on my twenty-first birthday. I still read them in astonishment and delight (and horror). I also discovered among the Baillieu's research collection, a folio of Black Letter Ballads, to which I usually knew the tune. Another kind of blunt verse, verging on bathos.

> *His throat they cut from ear to ear*
> *His head they battered in*
> *His name was Mr William Weare*
> *That lived at Lyon's Inn.*

If anyone is still haunted by a voice singing of murder and destruction in the Baillieu Research Collection, I can only apologise. It was not a ghost, it was *me*!

Throughout my university days, I bathed in words and stories; I frolicked in seas of narratives. So many books, so little time. I wanted to read EVERYTHING. Mrs Gaskell (whom I loved), Trollope (lukewarm), various Brontës (meh, except Anne), Thackeray, Wilkie Collins . . . the list could go on.

Meanwhile, I studied Legal History with a remarkable professor, Dr Ruth Campbell, who shooed me off to do my own research in my own field. I decided to discover all I could about the 1928 national wharf strike in Australia. My father was a member of the Waterside Workers Federation and helped me get access to the union's archives. I threw myself into the project, reading all the newspapers for that year, from the respectable

Argus to the highly dubious *Hawklet*. I fell in love with this original research. The newspapers told me not only what the parliament was debating in 1928, but also the price of eggs and what people were using to shine their floors (Shi-Noleum) and cure their colds (Canadiol Mixture) and perk them up (Dr Parkinson's Pink Pills For Pale People). I located three old men who had been on the wharves in 1928 and listened to them for hours. I drew maps and consulted directories, mining their memories for treasure.

At the end of my final term I had a paper written and square eyes. I got a gold star and an elephant stamp for my efforts, after which I put the manuscript away with all my novels, because I had worked over it for so long and loved it dearly.

'Nothing you learn is ever wasted', my mother always told me and she was, as is her habit, completely right. Not that I immediately noticed the potential of 1928 and a flapper hero called Phryne Fisher. Back then I was still writing about highwaymen and later about space adventures. I put all my research into a bottom drawer where it stayed until I finished my law degree and got a job at Legal Aid.

I was nearly 30. OLD, I thought. I had been writing since I was sixteen. It was high time I got published. So I sent my books hither and yon, to publishers and agents, hoping someone would love them as much as I did. I found that someone in Hilary McPhee, a wonderful editor, writer and publisher. She asked me to write a detective story with a female protagonist and said I could set it in 1928. I leapt at the poor woman and practically tore the contract from her hands.

Then I had to learn how to write a detective story, which I did in a completely ridiculous, unorthodox manner, for which I make no apology. But I should warn you—don't try this at home.

When I feel a book coming on, I get the same sense of doom as someone feeling that they are coming down with a cold. Bugger, I think, I haven't got time to be sick; I have a big project, or school play or Supreme Court appeal to organise. Then there's the party on Saturday that I really want to go to. But I already know that I won't be at the party, no matter how important it is or how offended the host will be. Thankfully, I have very patient, understanding friends. The impatient ones get weeded out fairly quickly.

Usually the muse manifests herself as a cross old lady with a black dress, hair skewered into a bun, pince-nez and a pointy nose. (I suspect I got her out of a nursery rhyme.) She pokes me in the back with a sharp fore-finger and says, 'Research South China Sea pirates' or equivalent.

I never know WHY I am researching the subject. The book hasn't formed yet. My muse is adamant and I must obey whether I'm investigating gay history, or the Magdalen Laundry at the Convent of the Good

Shepherd, or the trial of Oscar Wilde, or a boatyard in Williamstown, or a particular sort of cocktail.

I love research and this phase of the book process is benign. I might even get to that party, although I am likely to bore the arse off my interlocutors about my latest research. This phase may continue for a week, or perhaps a couple of months. The Ancient Egyptian novel *Out of the Black Land* took me a year to research, but I did get a trip to Egypt and also learned to read hieroglyphics.

Once my research is a critical mass, the next phase begins—the actual writing of the book. Surrounded by all my notes and photographs and books (which my partner says will one day undergo gravitational attraction and become a black hole), I begin to write. I still don't know what the book is about. I will have to write it to find out.

It doesn't matter if I am sick, tired, happy, on dialysis or in kidney failure, the book wants to be written and it will make me write it. It's a form of possession. Fortunately the Holy Office of the Inquisition is not active in my part of Footscray or I might find myself in real trouble, being handed over to the secular arm and burned at the stake at the Western Oval for consorting with devils.

Bewitched or otherwise, I have to write. Crippled hands. Melting with heat. Dizzy with migraine. It doesn't matter. I am required, compelled, to tell the story.

My novels always begin with a bang, sometimes

a literal bang—'the windscreen shattered'. I have always loved the way that ballads and Norse sagas leap into the middle of the story, which is why I plunge straight into the plot. Whatever it might prove to be.

Characters wander in and out. In my early days, I used to sternly excise ones who tried to take over. Now I know better. If the character is taking over, then they are meant to be the protagonist, whatever I (poor fool) might think. Sometimes I base characters on real people, which is easy. Corinna Chapman's building is stocked with my friends. Sometimes they just pop into my head, at other times they need to be fleshed out and made real.

The only imperative is that I MUST keep writing until the story decides to stop me, and then I go and do something else, because this is not a process that can be forced. Sometimes the words run out in the middle of a sentence, but this no longer worries me. There will be more words. There are *always* more words.

I have never written anything worth reading before 3 p.m. I start by reading what I wrote the day before, correcting spelling errors and cleaning up repetitions, the bane of editors. Then it's off again.

When I was young I used to be able to write a novel in three weeks. That was day and night and my wrists were stronger then. I would go into a trance, completely rapt in the unfolding story. It's a wonderful feeling but you do need someone to keep you fed. Now I have a censorious cat called Belladonna who supervises the process and won't let me write more than two hours without a break. She slyly hits the caps lock with her little black paw. Thus I am saved from carpal tunnel syndrome and she is well supplied with cat treats (those expensive green ones).

The book is heavy to begin with, a great weight on the shoulders, which ache under the burden. I frequently feel I could swap pointers with Sisyphus. Constructing the narrative, just getting all those words down on the page, is heavy going and hard work. But then there is the magic moment, when all of the clues have been embedded, though I don't know what most of them are for. From then on it is downhill and I fly after the story, typing, typing, typing as it unfolds. Characters speak. Run. Kiss. Puzzles are solved, sometimes in the last line. Oh, intoxication. It's so beautiful a process that I have typed pages with tears of joy running down my face.

As I warned earlier, please don't try this at home. This really is how I write novels, and I have more than 50 of them published, so I must be doing something right. But if you don't like writing classes (I could not have stood to have my work read aloud, especially at an early age), and you can't follow the 'plot, plan, paragraph breakdown' school of writing, then you might want to risk doing it my way. Stuff your head with as many books as you can read and at some point a story will discover you and demand to be told.

You can't get writer's block because when you haven't anything to say you don't write. This has led to many clothes being made and many jars of pickles on my pantry shelf. Housework is another great resource. Though when my partner, David, found me washing windows in the rain, he said, 'You're stuck, aren't you?' and I admitted that I was.

That was before I trusted the story to tell itself. I don't get stuck anymore. My method (if you can call it a method), brings to mind one of those Japanese paper flowers that look like nothing much until you put them in water and they unfold into myriad coloured petals. Or perhaps you can call it accretive, like a coral reef, where all the little polyps know exactly what shapes they should form.

Any process that produces a well-written novel is a good process.

MY RULES

1. *You need a place to sit that isn't shared by other people, especially children.*
You need time that is your own. These things are not negotiable. Write a sign for your door that says, GO AWAY in big black letters.

2. *Staring out of the window is working.*
You write from where you dream, not from where you think.

3. *Don't endlessly rewrite Chapter 1.*
Chapter 1 always has to be changed, because the finished book is not what you thought it was going to be. Keep writing until you have at least 20 000 words before you start altering anything.

4. The story wants to be told.

Let it talk to you. Follow it, even though it doesn't go where you expect it to go. It knows what it's doing. (Wrestling an obdurate story into a pretzel leads to tedious literature.)

5. Start by writing an imitation of your favourite writer.

It's a useful exercise. You are going to write more than one novel. You have to learn how you do it—just like riding a bike or staying afloat. More so than short stories, novels are a physical skill as well as a mental one.

6. I have a writing hat.

It is a tricorne made from an old felt hat I had as a student. It tells me that I am writing, when I am wearing that hat. When I stop writing, I take it off. Just like a barrister's wig says that he or she is in court. I recommend a writing hat. Or jacket. One of my novelist friends has fingerless gloves. The hat also tells anyone who drops in on me to go away.

7. The profession of being a writer is a solitary one.

You spend most of your writing time inside your own head, and you may be surprised at what is lurking there. If you don't like your own company, you could find writing a tad confronting.

8. You will miss birthdays, engagement parties, hens' nights, and (on one occasion) the wedding of a relative.

Prepare your friends.

9. You will have to ferociously defend your writing time,

which is why writing at night is a good idea if you don't mind the insomnia. People will assume that writing isn't a REAL job, which is why they'll ask you to mind their children, pick up their dry cleaning, volunteer for the tuck shop, supply a shoulder and tea and sympathy for their ruptured love life, take their mother to the dentist, or whatever. Warn everyone that you will not answer the phone or the door, ever, unless the house is on fire, or someone has died.

10. Back up everything.

I print out every chapter as soon as I finish it, so if my computer crashes or my hard drive fails, I will be able, however laboriously, to retype it or scan it. I thoroughly recommend any Apple computer. It has the personality of a large friendly dog—a labrador, say (though it has yet to jump up and lick my face)—and will not let me do terrible things, like closing a file without saving. And I am so old that I still proof pages, not screens.

11. Buy a biro and start writing.

Then keep writing.

FIVE MUST-READS

1. Bleak House *by Charles Dickens: Impelled by a ferocious zeal for social reform, Dickens still constructs a wonderful story, juggling several plots, and he wrote it in parts (the mind boggles).*

2. Bridge of Birds *by Barry Hughart: A beautiful, funny, bloodthirsty, clever evocation of Ancient China, memorable and remarkable.*

3. The Nine Tailors *by Dorothy L. Sayers: The best crime novel of its time. Nuanced, ingenious, and also has campanology.*

4. The Lord of the Rings *by J.R.R. Tolkien: Still the best and most believable sub-creation, bar none.*

5. The Three Hostages *by John Buchan: While working as an Attorney General Buchan dashed this off: three interlinked stories, all believable, funny, puzzling, a model for such things, which also cheekily contains a character explaining how such stories are made.*

Kerry Greenwood *is one of Australia's most celebrated and successful writers, best known for her Phryne Fisher historical mysteries, but also the creator of many other books, plays and children's stories. In 2003 she was awarded the Ned Kelly Lifetime Achievement Award.*

WHAT'S THE WORST THING THAT CAN HAPPEN?

by Geoffrey McGeachin

Most crime writing usually ends with the confession, but I want to turn that on its head. I hereby confess to having harboured a lifelong secret desire to be a published author—an ambition I managed to avoid by some nifty footwork until 'later in life' (by which I mean, nudging 50). Over many years, I found any number of excellent reasons to put off trying to write. The most common excuse I gave myself was that I loved *good* writing so much I didn't want to discover I was bad at it.

However, it's a well-known fact that 100 per cent of people who manage to get a book published have actually *written* a book. While actually writing a book doesn't guarantee you'll get published, it puts you several steps ahead of those who haven't.

Sounds easy enough, but you might be saying I don't have the time, or the right software, or an agent, or a BA in English literature or a garret in Tuscany. There are dozens of excuses for avoiding having a go. In the sophisticated and high-flying world of crime fiction we have a technical term for this sort of thing: bullshit!

My circuitous route to becoming a published writer started with reading. The exact moment that I discovered I could read was a sunny Sunday morning in the Wodonga Methodist church. I was self-consciously bluffing my way through a hymn, like all the other four- or five-year-olds when, bingo, the words in the hymn book suddenly made sense and I realised that when the congregation sang, 'Gladly the Cross-Eyed Bear', they weren't actually lamenting the woes of a teddy with strabismus. At that moment I fell in love with the magic of words and became a voracious reader. I realised words could entertain people, make them happy or sad, angry or concerned and could even make them laugh. I was hooked.

My dad was a bit of a quiet bloke, which made sense when I found out about his wartime service and some of the terrible things he'd been through. But he had a very dry Aussie wit and occasionally, when you least expected it, he'd drop a wry comment into a conversation. After a minute or two you'd realise the thoughts expressed in a few very carefully chosen words were not only pertinent, but also wickedly funny. It seemed that this playing with words business was a lot of fun and if my old man had the gene maybe I did too?

At seven or eight I started writing stories in school, usually humorous. The earliest I can remember concerned a town under attack by feral sandwiches. The hero escapes the carnage and has just locked himself in a room when someone knocks on the door, claiming to be a cop. 'You mean a police officer?' asks the hero. 'No,' comes the reply, 'I'm a cheddar, onion and pastrami sandwich.' (At this point I should remind you that I was only seven. Though, as you can see, I was already operating on quite a sophisticated literary level.)

In my second year of high school a substitute English teacher set us that classic essay topic, *What I Did on the Long Weekend*. My story started with a Saturday morning spent force-feeding my little brother breakfast cereal, jamming it down his throat like he was a Périgord goose. I was simply trying to collect a complete set of the plastic dinosaurs that came inside cereal packets and all those bloody cornflakes had to go somewhere! The essay continued on to describe in graphic detail the unexpected Sunday morning demolition of our back shed in a chemistry experiment gone wrong. Being a bit of a science buff and pyrotechnics enthusiast, the exploding shed part of my story actually had a basis in fact.

My completed essay was a tale full of pathos, food, fraternal combat and major special effects . . . almost Shakespearean in scope! (These days James Cameron and

Michael Bay would be bidding for the screen rights.) My name was called out in class, which always made me nervous, and I was asked to stand and read my essay aloud. Initially I thought that I was being singled out for bad writing. After a minute or two people started laughing and when the teacher joined in I realised I might be on to something. In a voice that rattled the classroom windows Mr Qualtrough-Sheffield announced: 'This boy has a great future as a writer.'

Now that *really* made me nervous. In the sixties in the northern suburbs of Melbourne, who knew what the hell that actually meant? Writers were, well, they were somebody else. And what if Mr Qualtrough-Sheffield was wrong? So I became a photographer instead, doing my storytelling with light, living in the United States and Asia, travelling to exotic locations, photographing lots of interesting stuff. Over the years the occasional wry comment or observation saw me offered jobs in advertising as a copywriter, or working on scripts for TV comedy shows, but I deftly kept sidestepping every writing opportunity thrown in my path! (Perhaps I was wrong not going into advertising since copywriting is apparently the second most lucrative form of writing. On a dollar return per word basis it comes in just after ransom notes.)

But in the back of my mind there was always this niggling idea about being a *real* writer. While living in Atlantic City, New Jersey, photographing casinos and mobsters and bikini girls on horseback high-diving into tanks of water, I found myself in a local bookshop one afternoon buying a copy of Robert Graves' classic, *The Reader Over Your Shoulder: A handbook for writers of English prose.* I guess I knew deep down that photography, casinos, mobsters and high-diving horses wouldn't be the sum of my creative life.

As it turned out, this photography caper had an upside for a future writer since the job came with a licence to watch. Photographers spend a huge amount of their careers just waiting: waiting for the right light, the right moment, the right expression. I sat on a Kowloon dock from four in the morning once, waiting while a red-painted Chinese junk slowly tacked its way up Hong Kong harbour under sail. Eventually it would cross in front of the luxurious five-star Mandarin hotel. The owners wanted a photograph of a traditional junk sailing past their hotel to use in a glossy advertisement and this was way before Photoshop. Six hours later, the junk was in the right spot for about 60 seconds and I got the shot, packed up and headed home. Later I would discover that those six hours on the Kowloon dock weren't wasted. All that sitting and waiting was perfect for people watching.

Almost unconsciously, I was listening and storing information away in the deep, dark recesses of my brain. Everything odd or interesting or disturbing or funny was added to the collection. I filed away situations and characters and reactions and turns of phrase and lots of other apparently useless stuff. Useless, until I became a writer who suddenly needed situations and characters and reactions and turns of phrase.

When I settled back in Australia and began teaching photography I discovered two things: first, that a written explanation of technical concepts seemed far easier for students to understand when I made it humorous. Second, that students were very risk-averse when it came to taking pictures for class assignments. They were afraid of taking bad photographs and having them criticised. It became my job to encourage them to take risks, to have a go, to see what they could achieve.

'C'mon, what's the worst thing that can happen?' became my classroom mantra.

I said this so often that I must have heard myself, because one day I decided to sit down in front of the computer and see whether I had what it took to be a real writer. After all, what's the worst thing that could happen? I might discover I can't write. I might not have a story worth reading. But on the other hand . . .

I've always been a joke-teller so I figured my story-telling would be in a humorous vein. In my first attempt, the hero is the manager of an about-to-close bank in a dying country town. He has an unfaithful second wife, two awful stepchildren who despise him and a weight problem from feeding his sorrows at the highway burger stop. And everyone has forgotten his birthday. He contemplates suicide twice before page 21, before robbing his own bank, shooting a bikie and teaming up with an ex-librarian recovering from a mastectomy. (Perhaps not what you might consider the basic ingredients for a humorous story or even a humorous crime story, but what might have been expected from the kid who once wrote 'Attack of the Killer Sandwiches'.)

At some point during this process, I began to realise I was having a terrific time writing. Even better, the results weren't too terrible. I began to relax and just go with it, to see where my characters led me . . . and lead me they did.

Once the manuscript was finished I needed an agent. Research suggested the ideal person, but she wasn't accepting new writers and her website said she didn't take unsolicited manuscripts. At that moment the NSW Writers Centre announced a national competition for a popular fiction book by an unpublished author. The competition was to be judged by this self-same agent and the first prize was representation, plus a guarantee of publication.

Just as you need to have written a book, if you hope to get one published, you also have to enter a competition to have any chance of winning. The entry details were announced online at nine o'clock on a Monday morning and by noon the Writers Centre had my hand-delivered entry. And out of 270 stories submitted mine was one of three shortlisted. A couple of months later, sick as a dog with the flu, I received news that my book had won and Penguin would be publishing it. It was the ideal moment for a medicinal whisky with honey and lemon juice but luckily we were right out of honey and lemons.

Suddenly I had an agent and a publishing deal. Soon I had the next prize—the buzz of seeing a book on the shelves with my name on the cover. No-one was more surprised than me, especially given the title: *Fat, Fifty & F***ed!* (which I never imagined they would use).

I'm a huge John le Carré fan, so with my second book I decided to try my hand at writing an espionage thriller. But I realised an Aussie spy story couldn't be told without humour. Remember, this is the country that once received an urgent fax from the French security agency, *Direction de la Surveillance du Territoire*, warning that a suspected dangerous terrorist was on our soil. The fax arrived late on a Friday evening before the Labour Day long weekend so of course ASIO was closed until 9 a.m. the following Tuesday. As the DST bods in Paris scratched their heads at our lack of response to their urgent warning on a matter of national security, our trusty ASIO operatives were out celebrating the achievement of the eight-hour working day at barbecues all over Canberra. (Willie Brigitte, the suspected terrorist, was quite possibly doing the same.)

In *D-E-D Dead!*, I created a fictional intelligence-gathering agency, which like all other government departments is full of smart, diligent, dedicated and hard-working people . . . and boofheads and time wasters and the odd no-hoper promoted way past his capabilities. Into this mix I placed our hero, Alby Murdoch, an Aussie sort of spy. Alby appeared in two more books, *Sensitive New Age Spy* and *Dead and Kicking*, still tongue-in-cheek but with a serious story underneath if you choose to go looking.

The Diggers Rest Hotel, my fifth book, was a definite change of direction, introducing Detective Charlie Berlin, along with some heavier themes and very dark moments. Despite the sombre subject matter, I was quite surprised to hear people commenting favourably on the humorous aspects because I hadn't realised there were any in there. (Maybe it is in the genes.)

Nine years on, from a standing start, I've had six novels published and won a couple of awards and nobody is more surprised than me. At the 2011 Ned Kelly Awards night in Melbourne—an evening I highly recommend—I know a lot of people were asking themselves, 'Who the hell is that bloke?' And I'll admit I was asking the same question.

It was only after the fourth book was published that I felt comfortable introducing myself as a writer and not a photographer or teacher who also writes. After book five and the Ned Kelly Awards, it became easier to introduce myself as an author or novelist. And when you do call yourself an author there is one question you always get: 'Where do your stories come from?' I remember seeing

Robert B. Parker on an American morning TV program where the interviewer, gushing about his prolific output as a writer, asked him where he got all his ideas. He gave an icy smile and said, 'I think them up.' Me too!

Stories and characters are all around us. Keep your eyes and ears open and pay attention. I usually begin by looking at a real situation or event and then ask myself, 'I wonder what would happen if . . . ?' And no matter how outrageous a concept I might come up with, odds are somewhere during the research phase it will probably turn up as fact.

I love doing the research part and would happily do it full time. Usually I do just enough to give me an overview of a basic event that allows me to run with the idea. As different situations come up in the writing process, I'll pause and do more research.

The trick with any research is to remember that less is always better. Don't try to cram a month's worth of your brilliant discoveries into a book just to justify the time and effort spent. If a month's research is refined down to a phrase, or word or gesture, that can be just as effective.

When I have the idea for the story worked out and have done enough research to satisfy myself it should work, I begin by writing the first and last lines. The opening line and that first page are where I want to hook the reader. Opening lines often pop into my head just as I wake up from a sound sleep or when I'm in the shower.

From that point I just have to fill in the space between the opening and closing lines, which is admittedly the tricky bit.

My routine used to be creative writing in the morning and revising in the afternoon. I'd start at five or six and then stop the creative part when someone spoke to me. (Fortunately my wife isn't a morning person and she doesn't like to form whole sentences before 9.30.) Now with half a dozen books under my belt I usually write anytime the sun is up.

A good plot is nothing without great characters. I have a quote pinned up above my computer saying: 'Plot is character in action'. Characters need to be as real as you can make them. Hanging out with a phony in real life is a waste of time and the same goes for your characters, major or minor. I need to believe in my characters as much as my readers do, believe they are real and that even the minor ones are off doing other things when they are not appearing in a specific part of a book. And a good character will often do and say things that I don't expect—and a smart writer lets them do it.

Early on in *Fat Fifty & F***ed!* there is a bit of banter between the hero and his best mate involving a regular joke about what a sentry should do if the ammunition dump blows up at midnight. 'Fire three shots in the air to alert the camp,' is the punch line. Months later in the writing process, the mate had to urgently send a simple, coded text message to the hero, warning him that the bad guys were closing in and he was in danger. That banter at the beginning let me use, '*BANG! BANG! BANG!*' as the warning message. I'd like to claim I planned it that way from the start, but I didn't—not consciously, at least.

For me, a very big part in creating believable characters is giving them their own voice; making sure they speak in their own way with their own rhythm, so that it's not my voice readers hear when a character talks. I find it really valuable to read all my work out loud as often as possible, and it's a great way to recognise written speech as opposed to spoken speech in order to make dialogue more organic and natural. This is even more important if your work is going to be made into an audio book; the narrator will love you for it.

As far as plotting goes I have a very loose plan but try to stay flexible and open to changes in direction. I allow myself to be carried along to see where the story goes and what the characters get up to. In *Blackwattle Creek*, the second Charlie Berlin story, a nuclear accident was a strong but minor plot point until around the fourth or fifth draft when I suddenly wondered, what if it wasn't an accident? This unexpected development gave the book an even more dramatic finish than I'd planned.

As a writer you are re-reading and rewriting, proof-reading and tweaking and cutting and agonising over your own words at least a dozen times before they hit the bookshops. If I couldn't enjoy what I'd written and still get the odd smile out of it now and again, then

I couldn't go on writing. The fact that other people seem to get pleasure out of what I do is just gravy.

So my advice for any would-be crime novelists out there is find something you think you'd enjoy writing about, stop making excuses and sit down at the computer and just do it. What's the worst thing that can happen?

Just do it. That's kind of catchy . . . snappy. Could almost be an advertising slogan. Maybe I should have had a go at that copywriting caper after all.

MY RULES

1. **Real writing is rewriting—**
   every writer knows this is true.

2. **Let your characters do what they have to do—**
   don't fight them.

3. **If you're going to write, write!**
   Don't just talk about it.

4. **Never trust spill check.**

5. **Learn everything, nothing is wasted.**

6. **Your editor is an advisor, not God.**
   It will be your name on the cover of the book not theirs. But you'd still be smart to listen to what they say.

7. **The Da Vinci Code *was Dan Brown's fifth book and first bestseller.***

8. **'Nothing succeeds as planned'—**
   from Good As Gold *by Joseph Heller.*

9. **Always listen to that little voice in your head**

   (except when it says, 'Kill them all!').

10. **Getting published will almost certainly NOT change your life in the ways you think it will.**

11. **Never having read Dostoevsky doesn't preclude you from becoming a writer**

    (but it can sometimes make things sticky on panels with 'real' writers).

FIVE MUST-READS

1. **Raymond Carver's short stories**

2. **Call for the Dead** *by John le Carré*

3. **The Reader Over Your Shoulder** *by Robert Graves*

4. **Dispatches** *by Michael Herr*

5. **Any of the titles by Geoffrey McGeachin** *or the other excellent writers who have contributed to this book*

Geoffrey McGeachin has worked as a photographer in advertising, travel, theatre and feature films and now teaches photography. His first novel, Fat, Fifty & F★★★ed! *won the inaugural Australian Popular Fiction Competition and was published by Penguin in August 2004. His fifth novel,* The Diggers Rest Hotel, *won the 2011 Ned Kelly Award for Best Crime Fiction.*
www.geoffreymcgeachin.com

WRITING GIVES ME WINGS

by Angela Savage

I had my first piece of writing published at the age of ten—a letter in a *Gould League* magazine in which I describe seeing a flock of Major Mitchell's cockatoos— exotic pink birds with flame-like crest feathers—roosting in the pine trees near our family home. They were actually the ordinary sulphur-crested variety, white with yellow crests, but I wasn't one to let the facts stand in the way of a good story.

That no one at the Gould League of Bird Lovers questioned how parrots native to Australia's arid and semi-arid inland came to be spotted in Melbourne's leafy eastern suburbs by a precocious ten-year-old taught me if your story is good enough, you can get away with murder.

You could say I was destined to write crime fiction.

Early on I made the assumption that to be a good writer, I needed to live an interesting life. So the year after I finished school, I left home for Paris to work as an au pair for an aristocratic French family. Ten months later, I was a seasoned traveller, fluent in French and completely convinced that I was a European trapped in the body of an Australian. I boarded the plane to fly home, believing it was only a matter of time before I'd be back in Europe. (I hadn't counted on the stopover in Bangkok.)

It was October 1985, my first experience of Thailand and of Asia. It blew my mind. *Farang* (foreigners) were still quite a rare sight in those days, so the Thai school-boys flocked around me when I stopped to have my photo taken at the Royal Palace. The *khlongs*—a network of canals that once saw Bangkok tagged as the 'Venice of the East'—were still the lifeblood of the city, where people drank, bathed, lived and traded. I was besotted, not least of all by the challenge of trying to get by in a place where blending in was not an option. It was the start of a love affair with Asia that continues to this day.

As an Arts student at Melbourne University in the 1980s, I wrote for the student newspaper, *Farrago*, and won its short story competition one year with a feminist fairytale inspired by my love of Angela Carter's purple prose.

During this period, I made a start on several novels, but didn't get far. I certainly never dreamed of writing crime fiction, although half of my Combined Honours degree was in Criminology.

In 1992 I won a scholarship to study in Laos. I left Australia for six months and ended up staying away for more than six years. Based in Vientiane, Hanoi and Bangkok, I managed HIV/AIDS programs for the Australian Red Cross and travelled extensively throughout Asia. My writing during this time was confined largely to sexual health education materials and project reports.

I started writing fiction again with a view to getting published when I returned to Australia from Asia in 1998. My experiences living, working and travelling in South-East Asia remain a major source of inspiration for my writing. Together with my partner, crime writer Andrew Nette, I continue to spend time in the region, and in 2008, we lived in Cambodia for a year with our then two-year-old daughter.

A large tax refund in 1998 made it possible for me to take time out of the paid workforce to focus on writing fiction. My first attempt at a novel was a thinly autobiographical account of an Australian twenty-something's experience of Laos in the early 1990s—big on textual detail but weak on plot. I consigned it to the filing cabinet and wrote short stories for a few months as a way of honing my plotting skills. One of these stories, 'The Mole on the Temple', inspired by a victim's account of a classic Bangkok card swindle, won third prize at the Sisters in Crime Scarlet Stiletto Awards that year, a modest success that put the idea of writing crime fiction into my head.

The more I thought about it, the more I realised crime was the perfect genre for the ideas I wanted to explore. Cultural misunderstandings are a rich vein for dramatic tension as well as humour, and working cross-culturally is a lot like being a detective. An outsider is always trying to figure out the big picture from a small set of clues; to distinguish a reliable source from one trying to take them for a ride; searching for meanings lost in translation.

I 'cannibalised' (to use Raymond Chandler's word) a couple of my short stories, plucking Bangkok-based Australian expat detective Jayne Keeney from 'The Mole on the Temple' to make her the flawed hero of my debut novel, *Behind the Night Bazaar*. As one reviewer said of Jayne: 'She smokes too much, speaks Thai fluently and likes a drink and a shag.'[1] She also has a well-developed moral compass and is unsentimental but not unaffected by her experiences.

Chiang Mai was the setting for *Behind the Night Bazaar*. I'd visited the northern Thai city several times, but it wasn't until a job with UNICEF took me back to Thailand in 1999 that the story idea came to me. Accompanied by a friend, I was distributing AIDS education materials in the bars behind the famous Night Bazaar shopping complex when I suddenly had a mental image of these bars deserted in the early hours of the morning and a young Thai cop stumbling across a badly mutilated body.

My initial manuscript was called *Thai Died*. The story was set in 1996 and drew on my experience dealing with AIDS, the sex industry, police corruption and the extraterritorial policing of child sex crimes. The manuscript was rejected by several publishers, but the rejection process delivered readers' reports that helped with further edits and, in 2004, I submitted a seventh draft to the Victorian Premier's Literary Awards. *Thai Died* won the prize for Unpublished Manuscript by an Emerging Victorian Writer. A member of the judging panel was an editor at Text Publishing and subsequently made me an offer. Four more drafts and eighteen months later, the manuscript was published as *Behind the Night Bazaar*.

My second novel, *The Half-Child* (Text, 2010), explores the ethics of overseas adoption and the layers of official corruption involved in adoption fraud. Though set in the sleazy Thai seaside town of Pattaya, *The Half-Child* was inspired by my experience of the booming inter-country adoption business in Vietnam in the mid-1990s. It was written in Phnom Penh in 2008, where

I befriended a number of expatriate women who shared their experiences of adopting Cambodian children. Their determination to ensure these adoptions were legal and ethical helped me to imagine what might be involved in illegal, unethical adoptions.

The third Jayne Keeney novel, *The Dying Beach*, is set on an exquisite stretch of the Andaman coast in Thailand's southwest. It was inspired by a combination of the setting and the work of Thai activists in the 1990s to strengthen environmental protections in the face of competing interests and official indifference.

Recently, in a shameless attempt to endear myself to the Australia Council for the Arts judges, I've been writing short crime fiction set closer to home. 'The Teardrop Tattoos', which won the Sisters in Crime Scarlet Stiletto in 2011, is set in Melbourne's inner north and was inspired by a chance encounter en route to my daughter's childcare centre. 'Killing Peacocks', which appears in *Crime Factory: Hard Labour* (Crime Factory Publications, 2012), is based on a true story that I relocated to the East Gippsland town of Cann River because it always struck me as the kind of place people go to disappear.

Writer Toni Jordan says there are two kinds of writers, plotters and pantsers: those who plot and those who fly by the seat of their pants. I am definitely in the pantser camp. I'll often start writing with little more than a scene, a character, a setting or an idea and seldom know how the story will play out, let alone what will happen in the end.

This approach has its pros and cons. I recall getting halfway through my first novel and hitting a brick wall until a writer friend wisely suggested I might want to do a little plotting to help things progress. On the other hand, halfway through the second draft of my second novel, the pantser approach gave me the freedom to radically change the plot for the better.

If I have a scene in my head that is particularly vivid, I'll write it down even if I'm not at that point in the chronology of the story. Some writers think this is heresy, but these scenes tend to be among the most vibrant and least reworked in the book. I will also skip scenes in the chronology if I feel uninspired and come back to them at a later time. Chances are if I am uninspired, the reader will be, too. It can help to step away and come back with a fresh perspective.

I value idle time and find twenty minutes' thinking can be more productive than a day in front of the computer. I really should think more often.

Martin Cruz Smith wrote *Gorky Park* without ever having visited Russia. For a novel with such a strong sense of place, it's an astonishing achievement. Maybe

I lack Cruz Smith's chutzpah, or maybe I'm aware that more of my readers are likely to have visited Thailand in 2012 than had visited Moscow in 1981 when *Gorky Park* was published, but I'm a firm believer in the value of field research. That it requires me to travel to exotic tropical destinations is just one of many ways I suffer for my art.

In writing crime fiction set in Thailand, I challenge myself to not only expose Thailand's seedy underbelly, but to also showcase the beauty of the country. I did this in *The Half-Child* by having a character come from Kanchanaburi, site of the infamous Death Railway built by Allied POWs and Asian labourers in 1943, and also home to some of Thailand's highest waterfalls and largest wildlife sanctuaries.

I visited Kanchanaburi in the early 1990s and have some vivid memories and amazing photographs of that trip. Back then I didn't keep detailed notes like I do now when I'm researching, so I did a lot of online research, reading old travel guides to fill in the blanks.

Based on my reading, I'd chosen the Tiger Cave Temple on a hill outside the town as a setting for a scene in the story. When I had the chance to visit Kanchanaburi again in 2008, I discovered that this temple is a major pilgrimage site with a fairground atmosphere not captured in the guidebooks. At the summit is a giant golden Buddha with an oversized alms bowl at his feet. People place coins in small trays on a conveyor belt that transports the offerings to the alms bowl. As Jayne observes in the novel, 'Low-tech, high-kitsch, gloriously Thai.'

I wanted to include the Tiger Cave Temple in the story, but not as the solemn setting for the scene I had in mind. As it happened, there was a much quieter Little Hill Cave Temple on an adjacent hill. So in *The Half-Child*, I had Jayne climb to the top of the Tiger Cave Temple, only to learn that the man she seeks is meditating at the temple next door.

Most of the action in the novel is in Pattaya, 'Thailand's own Sodom and Gomorrah', as one character calls it, a major R&R port. In the course of my research, I spent some memorable hours perched on a stool in a bar on Walking Street, taking notes on all that was going on around me: the people passing in the street as well as the girls and boys touting go-go bars, kickboxing and sex shows. I wanted to capture the sights, sounds and smells of the city. Many of these notes appear verbatim in the finished novel.

Despite the importance of good fieldwork, secondary sources can be just as valuable. After visiting Krabi province in 2009, I was determined to set a novel there. When I returned in 2011 to scope locations for *The Dying Beach*, it was only because I'd done the research that I knew what to look for. When I stumbled across a traditional bullfight (fairer than the Spanish version, in Thailand the bulls fight each other), I recognised it from my reading. And once I'd experienced the *hua chon* first hand, I knew I had to make it the setting for a scene in the book.

You're probably wondering why a writer who once thought nothing of substituting Major Mitchell's cockatoos for sulphur-crested ones would be so hell-bent on preaching the importance of research and attention to detail. For me, it's about getting enough right to make the story plausible. If it's real to me as the writer, it should be real to you as the reader.

As a fiction writer, it's my prerogative to make things up. I'll play with locations, time frames, distances, even geographical features when it suits me. My strategy is to get so many details right you don't notice when I make something up. Or if you do, you won't hold it against me.

They say you should write what you know, but I agree with Melbourne author Jeff Sparrow that such advice 'entirely misses the point of creativity'.[2] It's precisely what I don't know that inspires my writing—the allure of lives, cultures and places that are not like my own.

I don't know what it's like to be a Thai cop or a bar girl or a businessman, any more than I know what it's like to be an American marine, an evangelical Christian, an Indian-born IT geek or even an Australian Federal Police officer. That doesn't stop me from imagining

myself inside their heads. To write convincingly of characters across different cultures may put me on dangerous
ground, but with imagination and empathy, I aim to
get beyond the stereotypes and give my characters—
including the villains—depth and humanity.

On the subject of creating characters, I love what
Danish author Karen Blixen wrote in *Out of Africa*
(1937): 'To be lonely is a state of mind, something
completely other than physical solitude.' I feel less alone
when I'm by myself than any other time because it's
then I get to hang out with my characters, imagining
them into existence.

Some authors recommend writing detailed character
profiles, adamant that you should know more about your
characters than your readers do, but nothing delights me
more than having readers offer insights into my characters that haven't occurred to me.

I write intuitively. I've never studied creative writing,
but I've always been a voracious reader and I do believe
that reading well (and watching well-scripted movies)
makes you a better writer. You can learn much about the
elements of good storytelling by studying the masters of
the genre. I also believe that with writing, like any craft,
you get better with practice.

I have also learned a great deal from working with
editors when it comes to structure, plot and pace. My
first manuscript had 30 000 words cut from the draft at
the line-edit stage—a teeth-gritting exercise that gave

the final book more pace and edge. Second time around, at the same point in the editorial process, the cut was 3000 words, which shows how much I'd learned.

A risk with writing books like mine set in exotic destinations is they can tend towards travelogue, with lengthy descriptive passages that risk slowing the pace of the story. Unless the description serves to advance the plot or offer insight into a character, it has no place in the story. Much as it hurts, you must be prepared to kill your darlings.

I became a published author at about the same time that I became a parent. I was editing the galley proofs for *Behind the Night Bazaar* as my newborn daughter slept on my lap. The work–life balancing act has been at the forefront of my life ever since.

My current routine sees me combine writing with partnering, parenting and a four-day-a-week job in the community sector. I write four nights and one day per week. I am organised, disciplined, practical—not traits normally associated with the free-spirited life of an artist—and like Warren Zevon and Bon Jovi before me, I'll sleep when I'm dead.

If I could have a superpower, it would be the ability to bi-locate, to be in more than one place at a time—a gift allegedly possessed by twelfth-century Flemish Saint Drogo, who was seen simultaneously attending mass and working the fields. Needless to say, if I had the ability to bi-locate I would be neither at mass nor in the fields. I'd be writing and spending more time with the people I love.

Speaking of people I love, there are distinct advantages in living with another crime writer. Not only do we provide practical support to each other as partners in crime fiction, talking through ideas, plot lines and characters, reading and critiquing each other's work. We also respect each other's need for the time and space to write.

This work–life balancing act can be exhausting, but it's also exhilarating. I feel privileged to be able to write and sustain an artistic life amid other demands and passions. That said, writing full time remains my dream.

In his notes for this collection of essays, Michael Robotham posed the question: 'Is writing like pulling teeth or juggling hand grenades or jumping from a plane without a parachute?'

To that, I say: 'Writing gives me wings. Who needs a parachute?'

Endnotes

[1] Review by Jeff Glorfeld in the *Age*, 1 July, 2006. Accessed 25 June 2012, http://www.theage.com.au/news/book-reviews/behind-the-night-bazaar/2006/06/30/1151174384703.html.

[2] Working with Words: Jeff Sparrow, The Wheeler Centre, posted 14 June 2012. Accessed 24 June 2012, http://wheeler-centre.com/dailies/post/fd99db550db7/.

MY RULES

(WHICH ARE REALLY REMINDERS TO MYSELF)

1. **American writer Ray Bradbury, in a documentary about his great friend, special-effects wizard Ray Harryhausen, said: 'Ray and I learned at a very early age not to listen to anyone else, to focus on your passion, to burn it with your glance.'**

    That is my number-one rule. Forget about what everyone else is doing; focus on your passion, burn it with your glance.

2. **Do not feel compelled to write what you know.**

    Crime writers in particular should heed this advice. You don't need to commit murder to write about one. That's what your imagination is for.

3. **Make time for idle thoughts.**

4. **Resist the urge to rework the opening line/paragraph/ chapter.**

    The perfect opening may be the last paragraph you write. First get the story down.

5. **If a scene is vivid for you but you are not at that point in the drafting of your story, write the scene anyway.**

    Conversely, if a scene is giving you trouble then come back to it later.

6. **Carry something to write with/on at all times and eavesdrop shamelessly at every opportunity.**

    Take notes on dialogue, syntax, gestures, sights, smells and sounds.

7. **Don't use adverbs except in irony**

    (See use of 'shamelessly' in rule 6, above.)

8. Watch out for long descriptive passages that slow the pace of the story.

If a scene neither advances the plot nor provides insight into characters, cut it.

9. A great editor, like a great teacher, offers gifts to last a lifetime.

Cherish them.

10. Writing is a craft.

Learn from the masters. Hone your skills. Practise. And enjoy.

FIVE MUST-READS

1. Three Novels *by Raymond Chandler: These three classic Chandler novels,* **The Big Sleep** *(1939),* **Farewell, My Lovely** *(1940) and* **The Long Good-Bye** *(1953), are exemplars of American hardboiled fiction.*

2. The Song Is You *by Megan E. Abbott: This feminist take on classic American 1950s noir is both a stylish, mesmerising read and a horrifying exposé of the treatment of Hollywood starlets.*

3. Q & A *by Vikas Swarup: This sparkling debut novel by an Indian diplomat is even better than the award-winning film it spawned,* Slumdog Millionaire *(2008). Innovative in structure, the characters are nuanced and complex, especially the lead female, shamefully relegated to the role of prostitute in the film.*

4. The Judas Child *by Carol O'Connell: Dark, gripping and genuinely scary, just thinking about it sends a shiver down my spine.*

5. Private I. Guana: The case of the missing Chameleon *by Nina Laden: Leon the Chameleon is missing. Private I. Guana takes the case, trawling forest and swamp in his search. At the Lizard Lounge, 'a slimy place where only the most cold-blooded reptiles hung out', he finds Leon masquerading as Camille, a nightclub singer with house band the Gila Girls. When it comes to noir, I say learn 'em young.*

Angela Savage *is a Melbourne-based crime writer, who has lived and travelled extensively in Asia. Her first novel,* Behind the Night Bazaar, *won the 2004 Victorian Premier's Literary Award for an unpublished manuscript. She is a winner of the Scarlet Stiletto Award and has twice been shortlisted for the Ned Kelly Awards.*

A STRIPPING FEMINIST PRIVATE EYE

by Leigh Redhead

It was the Crazyhorse Adult Cinema that started the whole thing. I'd just moved to Melbourne after finishing a university degree in Sydney, majoring in the sort of subjects that ensure you'll never have to pay back your HECS debt, Creative Writing, Filmmaking and Cultural Studies. The BA was useless for securing a real job, but I could write a high distinction–earning essay about my vagina as a social space. As a result I was working as a banquet waiter at Crown Casino—possibly the shittiest hospitality position around.

On the way to the casino I'd pass the Crazyhorse on Elizabeth Street and always look up. It was damned hard to miss: lights flashed, speakers blasted Triple M's non-stop cock-rock and neon signs advertised 'Live Nude Peepshows' and 'Triple-X flicks'. Another sign declared, 'table dancing is for wooses', which annoyed me because surely they meant 'wusses'?

The stairs descended below street level and were lined with tiny, twinkling bulbs. Cheap air freshener wafted up as I passed, combined with cigarette smoke, the ammonia-filled scent of cleaning fluid and something more . . . how can I put it? Organic.

It was always funny watching men go in. They'd stride purposefully down the footpath, suit jackets flapping, eyes straight ahead, as though they were late for a business meeting or a train. Then, at the last possible second, they'd turn sharply and trot down the stairs.

I had done my share of dodgy work to pay my way through university. Lingerie waitressing. Erotic massage. But I had never been in a place like the Crazyhorse and wasn't entirely sure what went on inside. Was it just a front for a brothel? Were there blowjobs out the back? What exactly did you 'peep at' in a peepshow? I had no idea.

Another thing I noticed about the place was a sign behind the glass of the façade—right next to a life-size photo of a buxom eighties 'glamour' model sporting high-cut lingerie and a poodle perm. It was hand drawn in Texta, each letter a different colour: *Dancers wanted, any nationality, apply within.*

As each shift passed at my miserable banquet-waitressing job, the more obsessed I became with the mysterious, subterranean cinema. I'd always thought of

myself as an adventurous sort of chick. At seventeen,
I ran away to sea to work on a prawn trawler. If something frightened me, I'd usually make a point of doing
it, just to challenge myself, but the thought of walking
down those stairs scared the shit out of me.

One afternoon I left for work a little early, determined to go underground and ask about the dancer
advertisement. I tried the businessman's trick, striding
along and veering in at the last second, but chickened
out and had to do a couple of blocks before finally
summoning up the nerve. At the bottom of the stairs
I found a counter attended by a middle-aged woman
with emaciated eyebrows whose nametag identified her
as Rae.

'I'm here about the job,' I said. There was a black
curtain next to the counter and from behind it I could
hear the unmistakable 'ooh babies' and wet slapping
sounds of a porno flick.

'Worked the peeps before, love?' she asked.

'No. I did lingerie waitressing once, but I don't think
it's exactly the—'

'Here,' she said, holding out a two-dollar coin. 'Go
to one of the booths, stick that in the slot and come back
and tell me what you reckon.'

She pointed behind me. A glowing red 'Peepshow'
sign hung above the entrance to a corridor. Next to
it there was a second notice warning me not to enter
if sexually explicit entertainment offended. I slipped into

the first booth and gingerly pushed the accordion-style vinyl door open with my elbow, realising instinctively that it would be wise not to touch anything with my bare hands.

Inside, I made out a tissue dispenser, rubbish bin, and a metal box with a coin slot. A sign on the box advised that two bucks got you 45 seconds. As the coin clunked in, a window in front of me went from opaque to clear and revealed a small, round room lined with mirrors and illuminated by coloured disco lights.

In front of me a beautiful girl with Cleopatra hair wearing a red spangled bikini lolled back on a swivelling office chair. With a deft flick of her spiked heel she rolled right up to the window, slipped off the bikini top and ran her hands over her breasts, then moved to the bikini bottoms and slid them down to her thighs. Then the mechanism clicked and the vision was obscured. Right at that moment, if I'd been wearing a tie I would have loosened it.

I walked back to the reception area. Rae was leaning on the counter smoking a Horizon.

'Reckon you can do that?' She dragged hard on the cig, mashed it out.

'Yep.'

'So you want the job?'

'Shit yeah.'

It was true. Forty-five seconds of the girl behind the glass had sold me. I expected to see some seedy junkie or

154

crack whore, but the girl didn't come across that way at all. She had a regal, practically haughty expression, and flaunted the sort of sexual self-assurance I always wished I had. I was in awe of her. Hell, who was I kidding? I wanted to *be* her.

I had always wanted to write, even before I could read. My first story, 'The Farmer and the Ghost', had been dictated to my mother when I was three. Next up was a picture book shaped like an elephant that was actually *about* an elephant (genius). And when I was five I stayed up all night (it was probably 10 p.m. but it seemed like all night—the adults in the house had gone to bed) to finish a tale about a dinosaur brushing her teeth. It was never enough for me to just write the stories, though. They had to be read left to right and bound like a proper book.

I moved around a lot when I was a kid. My parents split up when I was young and my mum was variously a radical lesbian feminist, a heterosexual bohemian and a late-start hippy. I went to twelve schools in total and lived all around Australia and the world. Adelaide. Sydney. London. Munich. Los Angeles. We spent time in a commune called Amazon Acres where males over the age of twelve were banned, and an alternative community in Northern NSW where the kids ran wild, marijuana was the cash crop and the adults swapped partners with alarming regularity.

We were always on the fringes of society, living in city squats, converted buses or rural shacks with pit toilets and no electricity. I remember attending demonstrations and watching everyone get arrested. *Never* talk to the cops, I was told, while being given lessons on 'how to kick the pigs in the balls'.

One minute I'd be going to an alternative school—or no school at all—the next I'd be in some normal school in the 'burbs' with normal kids from normal families. Pretty soon the hippy kids thought I was straight and the straights thought I was a freak. It was hard to fit in, which actually is a pretty good thing for a writer. I spent a lot of time on my own, observing people, reading and writing.

What I loved to read was crime fiction. I was obsessed with the Trixie Belden girl detective series. Trixie was a grubby tomboy from the wrong side of the tracks who constantly messed up, but always solved the mystery. My favourite book was *The Mystery of the Unseen Treasure* in which Trixie and her mates stumbled across a dope crop hidden in a cornfield. They burn some to have a smell and get seriously busted for stinking of pot! (Now that I think about it, the hero of my crime series, Simone Kirsch, is just like Trixie—if you imagine Trixie growing up with a bunch of hippies and finishing up working in a titty bar.)

So I was a crime fiction fan from a young age, but when I hit thirteen, I strayed from the path of righteousness.

I started reading literature with a capital L. There were a couple of reasons for this. First I knew I wanted to be a writer some day and I thought that's what you had to do—read a lot of serious, dense, worthy stuff. Of course I had no idea what ranked as 'worthy', so I'd go down to the bookstore or the library, check the back of the book to see if the author had won a Nobel Prize for literature. If they had, bingo, I'd buy it or borrow it. I figured if it was good enough for the Nobel judges, it was good enough for me.

Second, I started going to Wingham High, a country school an hour away from the alternative community where I lived. They thought we were hippies, and we thought they were rednecks. The most uncool thing you could do at Wingham High was read books when you didn't have to. It was way cooler to go down the Wingham brush and smoke cones, or be on the footy team, or go to a party on Sat-dee night and vomit passion pop everywhere. (Or, if you were a guy, it was also cool to 'root chicks', but if you were a girl getting rooted meant you were a slut.)

'Reading? Who do you think you are? Some kinda brainwave?'

I knew I'd never fit in, so I took a perverse pleasure in being the complete outsider, wandering the quadrangle pretentiously with a Gabriel García Márquez or Patrick White under my arm. No wonder I couldn't get a boyfriend.

When I left school unemployment rates were sky-high, and the only work I could find was on a prawn trawler fishing from Cairns to Cape York. I was to be a cook and deckhand and we were going out to sea for three months without setting foot on land. No radio, no TV. I went to the bookshop before we left. What better opportunity would I have to finally read *War and Peace*? I didn't read a word of Tolstoy. Instead I found a box under one of the bunks full of pulp fiction (not to mention a pile of *Picture* magazines). Suddenly I had action, adventure, plot twists, thrills and sleaze. I was back to crime!

I spent my entire twenties addicted to this sort of stuff. If someone didn't die a hideous death in the first 50 pages, I didn't want to know about it. I read all the serial killer books by the likes of Patricia Cornwell and Thomas Harris, but got sick of them pretty quickly. I mean, where's the motivation? The characters are serial killers. They're sick puppies. It's just what they do. I became more interested in reading stories about ordinary people who resorted to crime. What drove *them* to such extremes? What was *their* motivation?

Occasionally, I dabbled in police procedurals, which were okay, but the characters, being cops, were a little straight for my liking. Then I got into PI books and I absolutely loved them. Peter Corris, Marele Day, Raymond Chandler, Sue Grafton. As a reader, I had the pleasure of working out not only who committed the

crime but more importantly why. And after my uncon-
ventional upbringing, I guess I related to characters who
operated outside the law. Noir thrillers also appealed
to me, although I always wanted the femme fatale to get
away instead of being punished at the end.

So there I was at the Crazyhorse, working as a peepshow
girl. Despite the sleazy trappings the work was fun.
I lost a few friends along the way—the ones who couldn't
understand that being a feminist and a stripper weren't
mutually exclusive—but I made new ones. The other
dancers were friendly, bawdy and funny as hell, and each
shift was a combination of playing dress-ups and putting
on a high-school musical, albeit a raunchy one. You
could do anything you wanted on stage: tell a story; take
the piss out of yourself or the crowd; perform a comedy
act to crack up the other girls.

Every day something ridiculous happened. One time
a guy carked it in the cinema, and no-one realised he
was dead for eight hours. When the girls complained
that he smelled the cashier sprayed him with air freshener. (Okay, maybe that isn't so funny. Either that or you
had to be there.)

As much as I'd wanted a grown-up job after university, possibly with a suit and a briefcase, I realised I'd
actually fallen into the perfect occupation for a wanna-be
author. I worked good hours and was gathering material

every day. I got to know strippers who were mothers and students, party girls or personal trainers. I met bikies and gangsters, swingers and corrupt cops, blue-collar workers and businessmen. I was privy to their hidden lives and secret fantasies.

Of course I still wanted to write. I enrolled in a professional writing course at the Melbourne CAE, and took Novel Writing 1. I began writing about a stripper called Simone (my dancing name) with a working title, *Peepshow*. You're probably thinking this was a crime novel, right? Noooo. In some weird hangover from my days at Wingham High, I saw myself writing a literary novel. Simone didn't do much in *Peepshow* except loll about, pondering her Brazilian and her existential angst. Needless to say it was a boring piece of shite.

Then I attended a session at the Melbourne Writers Festival called 'Why Write Crime?' featuring Kinky Friedman, Robert Crais and some Australian guy who seemed to be quite drunk. They basically said, 'Why would you write anything else? You can still have serious issues in a crime novel, but you wrap them up in an entertaining plot and get your point across all the more effectively.'

Talk about a 'eureka moment'. *Peepshow* had to be a crime novel. How could I have been so stupid? On the tram on the way home I tried to think of a crime. I went through a mental hit list I had been keeping for years. Top of the pile was the sleazy boss of a King Street table-dancing club. I immediately went home and wrote a scene where his body washes up on St Kilda beach. Simone Kirsch, feminist stripper and fledgling private investigator, was born.

I've written four Simone Kirsch novels now. The idea for each one comes from a combination of setting and wanting to expose a particular issue or explore some aspect of human nature. I also have a desire to work through my list of people who have pissed me off. I usually disguise them just enough to avoid getting sued, then turn them into either the murder victim or the villain of the piece. I can't tell you how satisfying this is, which is why crime writers are the loveliest and most chilled out people you will ever meet.

The plot usually comes about because of the inter-action between characters. The inhabitants of my novels come from anywhere and everywhere, but end up as an amalgam of myself, friends and people I've known well or met briefly. Horrible people are a boon for crime writers, as are disastrous social situations, and I'd encourage everyone who wants to write crime to expose themselves to both.

At dinner parties sit next to that guy who no-one can stand. Steal his dialogue and try to analyse why he's so offensive. What's the psychology behind him and the reactions he creates? Another good idea is to put a little bit of yourself into every antagonist. Try to remember when you've been bad (or at least thought about it). When have you felt greed, lust, rage or the desire for revenge?

I start each book by free writing in longhand in hardcover notebooks that I lug about everywhere. I get lots of writing done on public transport. I can't procrastinate on the Internet and there's something about the motion of trains that sends me into a creative trance. This is great because most days I would rather do anything but write. The words rarely flow and I have to force myself to stick to a daily word count—usually one to two thousand words.

I fill up about four of the notebooks with a huge, crappy, rambling draft that is part novel, outline and journal. I never show it to anyone except writing students. Look, I say, if this awful mess can become a book then you guys have nothing to worry about.

I type the second draft into the computer, and then the third, and the fourth. It takes me multiple drafts to figure out the plot, which is a shockingly inefficient way to work and I'm trying to become a planner, so far without success. I write best first thing in the morning, coming to the desk straight from sleep with a plunger full of coffee by my side.

Setting my books in backgrounds I'm familiar with means that half my research is done. Strip clubs. Massage parlours. Hotels. Casinos. Writers Festivals. Alternative communities. I usually leave technical details until later drafts because research can easily become procrastination (it's a waste of time figuring out the minutiae of some gadget or point of law if the scene ends up being cut).

I did a private investigator's course while I was writing *Peepshow*, which was really helpful. The instructor was an ex-undercover cop who had worked as a PI for years and had fabulous stories, some of which I pinched. As part of the course I had to tail someone for eight hours and came to realise exactly how difficult it is to have a leak using a combination of a juice bottle and a funnel.

Peepshow wasn't published until I'd moved from Melbourne to Mullumbimby. I joined the Northern Rivers Writers Centre, which had an annual mentorship where you could submit the first 50 pages of your novel and, if selected, spend a week working on it with Marele Day. I loved Marele's Claudia Valentine PI series and was desperate to get into the mentorship program. Luckily, I was accepted and was able to send the reworked pages to Marele's publisher, Allen & Unwin. They liked what they saw and eventually agreed to publish *Peepshow*. My childhood dream had finally come true.

I was so excited I called everyone I knew, but no-one was home. I celebrated anyway—with copious quantities of a four-litre cask, which was all I could afford at the time. (I was working as a six-dollar-an-hour apprentice chef.)

I much prefer being a crime writer to working in the kitchen. One of the best things is getting to meet other crime writers I admire from Australia and around the world. I'm always star-struck at first, but they're without exception friendly, generous and down-to-earth. There aren't many downsides to the profession—except perhaps for sitting next to Matthew Reilly on a signing table, or having your grandparents read your sex scenes.

So God bless the Crazyhorse. I've never regretted swerving down those stairs.

MY RULES

1. **Write every day, even when you don't feel like it.**

2. **Jump straight into the action on the first page.**

3. **Don't have a goody-two-shoes as a main character.**

4. **Make sure your protagonist drives the action and is not rescued by someone else at the end.**

5. **Have some sort of conflict in each scene.**

6. **Describe people, places and things using specific detail.**

7. **Know your characters' darkest secrets.**

8. **Give your characters believable motivation for acting the way they do.**

9. **I've always liked the saying:**
   'What is there at the beginning should be there at the end, utterly transformed.'

10. **Be insecure.**
    Writers who think they're shit hot are usually bloody awful.

FIVE MUST-READS

1. **Miami Purity** by Vickie Hendricks
2. **Queenpin** by Megan E. Abbott
3. **The Cutting Room** by Louise Welsh
4. **Pop. 1280** by Jim Thompson
5. **Any of the Cliff Hardy PI series** by Peter Corris

Leigh Redhead's first novel, Peepshow, *burst onto the crime fiction scene in 2004 introducing stripper turned private investigator Simone Kirsch. Simone has continued to thrill readers in* Rubdown, Cherry Pie *and* Thrill City.
www.leighredhead.com

FIRST FIND SOME ATMOSPHERE

by Barry Maitland

I'm always astonished, listening to other crime writers explaining their craft, by the extraordinary variety of ways they say they go about it. Some plan meticulously before they start writing, like James Ellroy who prepares a detailed outline, longhand on legal pads, several hundred pages long. Others say they sit down to write each morning in front of the computer without any idea of where the story will take them that day. So it seems that we all have to find the way that suits us, and my way is to start by discovering the place in which the story will happen.

This may seem an odd way to begin. Surely character and plot are more important than setting? Yet for me the scene of the story holds the key to all the other crucial things that need to be developed. I look for places—real places—that intrigue me. That's where I'll find authentic characters whose stories interest me. For people and the things that happen to them are shaped and conditioned by the places in which they live and work.

We as humans are highly attuned to this, immediately sensing the atmosphere as we step through a front door or stray into an unfamiliar district. And it is this question of *atmosphere* that lies at the heart of my choice to begin with place. The crime fiction I most admire is steeped in atmosphere, whether that of James Lee Burke's Louisiana, Sara Paretsky's Chicago, Michael Dibdin's Italy or the Nordic gloom of the Scandinavian authors.

Beginning with atmosphere has always been my approach, but I've since discovered that some of my favourite crime writers have adopted the same methods, including Georges Simenon, whose stories had always seemed so highly spontaneous and unstructured.

Simenon writes: 'I first find some atmosphere. Today there is a little sunshine here. I might remember such and such a spring, maybe in some small Italian town, or some place in the French provinces or in Arizona, and then, little by little, a small world will come into my mind, with a few characters.'

Atmosphere also plays a great part in the foundation texts of crime fiction. When Edgar Allan Poe introduced us to his detective, C. Auguste Dupin, in *The Murders in the Rue Morgue*, he began not by describing the man but where he lived, in 'a time-eaten and grotesque mansion, tottering to its fall in a retired and desolate portion of the Faubourg St Germain'. Immediately, we have a sense of the character and the story that is to come.

Similarly, in our first sighting of Sherlock Holmes in *A Study in Scarlet*, Arthur Conan Doyle showed us not what he looked like but where he was to be found, in 'the wing of a great hospital, ascending a bleak stone staircase, through a low arched passage, into the chemical laboratory, a lofty chamber lined and littered with countless bottles'. This gives us a taste of Holmes more vivid than any description of his clothes or appearance.

So I begin with place, and it is only when I can visualise it clearly, its streets and buildings and weather, that I can begin to create that 'small world' that Simenon speaks of. I picture the characters that live and work there, and imagine their relationships, their problems and the murders they will commit. I did this instinctively with my first crime novel, remembering a small street in London's West End called Cecil Court, lined with antiquarian bookshops, in which, as a student, I had once found a rare document, and which became the genesis of *The Marx Sisters*.

With each successive book in the series I then went on to explore other promising corners of London, some wealthy, some impoverished, some familiar, others obscure, but all, to me, full of character and atmosphere. I studied shopping malls, stately homes, inner- and outer-city suburbs, the area around Brick Lane in the

East End where Pakistani immigrants have settled, and in Brixton in South London, not far from where I went to school, where West Indian immigrants gathered.

Some of these places I remembered from growing up in London, but years later I was revisiting them as a 'foreigner', rediscovering them as they are now, changed by time, so that the London growing in my mind was part memory, part new reality and part imagination.

In looking into those places I came upon certain possibilities for additional themes that were often unexpected and intriguing. One of the great things about murder stories is that the detectives can open any door and delve into any life. In this way any and all of the quirks and strange compulsions that grip people are exposed. Thus in each of my books some theme has emerged that grew out of my research into its characters and place. It might be the practice of naturopathic medicine, the forgery of rare stamps, the celebrity focus of contemporary art, or the claustrophobic world of the theatre.

I have a particular liking for themes and stories that have a historical dimension, a sense of the roots of the crime extending back in time, perhaps a few years, perhaps a hundred or more, so that the investigation of a contemporary murder takes the detectives on an almost archaeological search back through layers of people's lives.

Historical stories woven into my novels have included the life and strange suicide of Karl Marx's daughter, Eleanor, in 1898; the exodus out of Jamaica to London, New York and Toronto in the 1960s and 1970s; the incidence of arsenic poisoning at the time of the Pre-Raphaelite painters in Victorian England; and the reverberations of old Cold War history in the move of rich Russians to live in London in recent years. Many of these stories contain real unexplained mysteries from the past and I love the possibility of linking these lacunae to a contemporary crime, which I think can give a richness and density to the novel.

This backward trail also suggests an interesting structure of two overlapping storylines, one moving forward in time as the investigation proceeds, and the other backward as the detectives probe deeper into the origins of the crime. These sequences are happening simultaneously, with the possibility of each illuminating or disrupting the other.

So far so good. We now have places, characters, potential story lines, themes and possible histories—a lot to research and become totally confused by. How do we turn all this into a strong, coherent novel of about 100 000 words, with tremendous pace, culminating in a stunning, unexpected climax?

I wish I knew.

For me, the process is not a predictable linear path to be followed, but rather a struggle marked by periods of groping in the dark in complete confusion and despair. There are, however, some guidelines. One that has some resonance with me is the scheme put forward by Henri Poincaré, a brilliant French mathematician who discovered a host of astonishing results, and in the process became intrigued by the way his own mind worked. How did it come up with all this stuff? In 1908 he described what he thought was going on in a lecture to psychologists in Paris. These ideas were later set out by another polymath, Graham Wallas, in his book, *The Art of Thought*, in 1926, in which he described the stages that you go through in a creative process.

Preparation

This is where your mind focuses on the problem. For a novelist this means research, visiting locations, reading, talking to people, sketching out character profiles, plot lines, themes, and so on. Importantly, it also means thinking about what the book is *really* about. Eventually, this accumulation of research becomes overwhelming. You feel like the detective in your story: confused by contradictory information and unable to see the way forward. So you move on to stage two.

Incubation

You close the door of your writing space and do something completely different, maybe physical, like a long walk or digging the garden or building a shed, or playing snooker in the pub, or listening to music. I know it won't *look* as if anything is happening, but according to Poincaré and Wallas the problem is being internalised and absorbed by your unconscious mind (tell this to your spouse/agent/editor who are wondering what you're up to). I call this mulling.

Illumination

It may be a sudden miraculous 'eureka moment' where you wake up in the middle of the night knowing exactly what to do, or it may be a quieter revelation, returning to your writing space one day and realising that everything seems much clearer.

Think of your brain as a compost heap (bear with me on this) you have piled in all that disparate material to and then walked away from, unable to see how it would ever make anything worthwhile; then you come back and find that, amazingly, it has been transformed into a wonderfully rich, homogeneous, fertile humus. Well, that's the theory. Now you have enough confidence to start to write. When you get to the end you move on to the final stage.

Verification

In an author's case, this means re-reading, checking, rewriting, letting someone you respect have a look at it, thinking, rewriting, editing and rewriting.

I must confess that my writing doesn't fall into four neatly compartmentalised stages like this, but rather is an iterative process, going through that preparation, incubation and illumination cycle again and again as the writing proceeds. This is perhaps because the creation of a novel is a comparatively long project, and the writing stage is itself a process of discovery, as characters become clearer and unexpected plot possibilities reveal themselves.

Apart from avoiding panic and writer's block, the incubation stage has an important function in relation to research. One of the great appeals of crime fiction to me is its sense of authenticity and its history of constantly reinventing itself to reflect contemporary problems and realities. This means investigating how things actually work through observation and research.

When I wrote my first crime novel this was quite difficult, and meant having access to people involved directly in the process. This was one of the reasons I set that first book in London, where I knew people in the police force and in forensic science, who could tell me how things were done.

Today I can review the latest developments in the law, or changes to the organisational structure of the London police, or watch the scene in London streets live, and do a host of other research tasks without leaving my computer. The Internet has made access to research material so easy there is a danger that the novel becomes overloaded with interesting stuff that I've discovered and the characters become mere ciphers for conveying research information.

This is where the *incubation* stage comes in. It's worth remembering that Poincaré was a mathematician who scorned logic and rigour. He considered his own mental processes to be intuitive and visual. We also have to remember that we're writing fiction, an imaginative invention, not a documentary. This is why the incubation stage is key to our absorbing and digesting our research and allowing us to make it subservient to the artistic project of the novel.

Although I may begin with real places and model characters on real people, I soon find that I have to fictionalise them for the purposes of the story. Place, characters and plot are all inter-dependent and develop together, affecting each other.

The Marx Sisters began when I imagined Cecil Court, but soon I realised that I needed a synagogue at one end, then a tube station at the other, and that it would work better if the lane cranked and widened in the middle to create a small square where the characters could meet up. In this way Cecil Court became transformed into Jerusalem Lane. Years later I got a letter from an Italian reader who had read *The Marx Sisters*, and wanted to tell me that he knew that street so well. It was in Bloomsbury, he said, and he had met his first great love there.

After reading the novel he had taken his wife (not his first great love) back to show it to her.

It was a wonderful letter, but he was wrong about the street. Yet I knew immediately that Jerusalem Lane had captured some essence of a London street that had come to life for him.

Again, in *Babel*, I started with the real Brick Lane then discovered that I needed a second mosque, and a Yemeni café in a side street, and gradually it became transformed into a fictional place, Shadwell Road. Recently I returned to Brick Lane, and was shocked by how drab and uninteresting it seemed compared to the vibrant Shadwell Road in my head. In the same way, Qasim Ali, the Yemeni owner of the Horria Café in my story, seemed far more vivid and alive than the people I saw hurrying down the real Brick Lane.

At that moment I realised that he *had* come alive in my imagination, not because I had written a brilliant individual portrait, but because of how he had struggled to assert himself against other characters in the story.

Maybe there's something a bit strange about creating people and places in your head that are more real than the ones you see around you. Perhaps, DSM IV, the Diagnostic and Statistical Manual of Mental Disorders (more research) has a classification for it.

But if I don't believe in my characters, how can I expect my readers to believe in them?

Good luck.

MY RULES

1. Write, and write and write.

2. Read, and read and read.

3. Begin, if possible, with a compelling proposition.

4. Pace is crucial in crime fiction and this reality should stop an author from being self-indulgent.

5. Dreams.

Don't. I once asked an agent how she managed to get through all the manuscripts she was sent, and she said that the first cull came as soon as a character started describing his dreams. (Actually there have been some brilliant books about dreams—The White Hotel by D.M. Thomas, comes to mind—but better not try it.)

6. Details.

Caress the detail, the divine detail (Nabokov). God is in the details (Mies van der Rohe).

7. Clichés.

It's very hard to avoid clichés in writing crime fiction. They lie in wait for you everywhere—characters, plot lines, language. Re-read your work with your cliché meter turned up high.

8. End with a stunning twist if you can, but take your time.

After having got so far there's a tendency to rush to the finish. Give yourself space to do justice to what's come before.

FIVE MUST-READS

1. **Bleak House** by Charles Dickens

2. **The Great Gatsby** by F. Scott Fitzgerald

3. **Inspector Maigret and the Killers** by Georges Simenon
   (or one of his many others)

4. **The Spy Who Came in from the Cold** by John le Carré

5. **Atonement** by Ian McEwan

Barry Maitland is the author of the acclaimed Brock and Kolla series of crime mystery novels set in London, where Barry grew up and studied architecture at Cambridge University before moving to Australia in 1984. His novel The Malcontenta *was joint winner of the inaugural* Ned Kelly Award for Best Crime Fiction.
www.barrymaitland.com

BEAUTY AND DEATH

by Tara Moss

For me the obsession began early. At the ripe old age of ten, in the quiet, green suburbs of Vancouver Island, I was making off with Stephen King novels from the local library to read under the covers of my bed by torchlight while my parents believed me to be asleep. *Christine*, *Cujo* and *Carrie* all thrilled me. By all accounts I was a gruesome tomboy as a child, obsessed with horror, magic, ghosts and dragons. Before long my obsession with those stories made me want to write them. I took to any notebook I could find to jot down the stories swirling in my head.

One of my earliest tales was a Stephen King–inspired 'novelette' called *Black and White Doom*, featuring a *Christine*-style homicidal, demonically possessed car that systematically killed off my classmates. The death scenes were long and drawn out, and sometimes came with illustrations. Now, before you jump to any conclusions about sinister motives, my classmates at school—all equally morbid—asked to be written in and killed off and would wait until after class to get the handwritten chapter featuring their own grisly demise. Such is the morbidness of ten-year-olds, I suppose.

Next I graduated to Choose-Your-Own-Adventure-style tales featuring wizards and dragons and all sorts of exotic monsters, described in my careful childhood prose and decorated with sketches of skeletons and ghouls. Again my classmates waited eagerly for each new instalment. Every chapter featured a plot twist and ended with the reader having a choice to make— *Venture into the dark cave and seek the treasure at the risk of a vicious dragon? Or retreat back to the castle?*

As I became obsessed with Ray Bradbury, science fiction plots found their way into my scribblings, again featuring cliff-hanger chapters and dreadful denouements. My father collected these stories and stored them in the attic for years. When my first novel, *Fetish*, was published in 1999, he sent some to me. I had forgotten those early writings, but have since taken to reading sections of *Black and White Doom* at literary conferences from time to time, usually introducing it as 'some of my early work'. There is often a bit of confusion when I get to the bit about the 'dismantled hand'. (I meant dismembered, but hey, I was ten.)

To this day I consider Stephen King the writer who made me want to become a novelist. From those first moments that I read him beneath the covers by torch-light, I knew that I wanted to write, wanted to take people on the same journey of fear and intrigue. Yet by the time I became a teenager, my childhood confidence had evaporated and the idea of showing my stories to anyone was terrifying.

I was 23 before I showed another soul something I had written. In the intervening years, I continued to read and to write obsessively. By then I was modelling to pay the bills, and writing in between fashion shows and photo shoots. My abiding memory is the total dis-interest shown by people when they asked me what I was doing and I told them about the novel I was working on. The subject would change as if I had not even answered. No-one gave 'a rats', to use the Austra-lian parlance.

To say that I had little support in the beginning would be putting it mildly. I didn't have an agent or a publisher. Even my boyfriend at the time, who was something of a Luddite, couldn't fathom why I'd bought a computer with my savings, and was tapping away at the keyboard regularly. (This was in the 1990s, before everyone had a computer, an iPad, etc.) For me, the idea of being published was still very abstract back then. Being an author was something I dreamed of, but did not expect to achieve. (In many ways, I still write for myself, which is perhaps one of the keys to writing with authenticity.)

Eventually, I got up the courage to take a correspondence course at the Australian College of Journalism, and the tutor, Marg McAlister, was fantastic. The course helped me to organise my ideas. Soon I entered a contest called the Scarlet Stiletto Awards, organised annually by Sisters in Crime, a group I am still involved with. The awards are for women's short crime fiction and they are judged blind. That last detail appealed to me a great deal. If my writing turned out to be terrible, no-one would know it was mine.

I won the Scarlet Stiletto Young Writers Award that year, and got the attention of my agent, Selwa Anthony, who has represented me ever since. When I finished writing my first novel, *Fetish*, I sent it to Selwa and three major publishers began bidding for it. HarperCollins published it in 1999 and my childhood dream had come true . . . or so it seemed.

For those of you reading this who dream of being published, let me warn you: it can be a daunting experience as well as tremendously exciting. It's natural to have mixed feelings about it—the critics, the unprecedented exposure, the idea that your months or possibly years of hard work are now in the spotlight.

My first three years as a published author were doubtless the most difficult personal time in my life, not counting the loss of my mother when I was a teen.

Let me explain.

Writing my first novel had been difficult—novels always are—and being published in 1999 at the age of 25 was a dream come true. But I was not fully prepared for the reaction I was to receive. *Fetish* received a lot of attention and any author would be foolish not to be grateful for this (authors' careers are far more likely to die of obscurity than from bad reviews). However, I found myself the target of unsubstantiated rumours of heavy editing or ghostwriting.

Essentially it went like this: a) the book can't be any good because a model wrote it, and b) I bet she didn't write it anyway.

I had been modelling to pay my bills since I was sixteen, and I was largely unaware that anyone took the stereotypes about models seriously. Modelling is a job. It pays a lot of young people's way through university. And how exactly does physical appearance indicate intellectual ability? (Think Sharon Stone's 'Mensa' status, or Stephen Hawking.)

The accusations were never made to my face, of course. I was made aware of them from friends, from other authors, and later, from my own publishers, as they gradually heard about the swirling rumours. I recall a high-profile article on ghostwriting that mentioned the at-the-time recent revelation that Naomi Campbell had not written her novel, *Swan*. The same article mentioned that I was a model who had just put out a novel. The implication was clear.

The zenith of this foolishness was a cover story in the *Weekend Australian* in 2002 when I was dared to take a polygraph test to prove that I wrote my own novels. I passed and as a bonus I now have a 30-page report declaring what I already know. 'Guilty as charged, I am an author,' I said afterwards. The rumours seemed to fall away after that and I was able to laugh about it. Looking on the bright side, I am perhaps the only scientifically proven author in the world.

Thirteen years and eight novels later, it seems rather absurd, but at the time, in a world before social media and blogging, there really wasn't a lot that an ex-model who was new in the writing world could do about rumours and assumptions. I did what came naturally to me. I kept writing.

Even now, I am still not a methodical planner. I tend to think about a novel for a long time before I write the first words, so that I have a solid idea of what I'd like to see on the page, but the story naturally evolves through the process of physical writing. I believe the book is boss. It will tell me where it wants to go. The characters and their stories take over. No editor has a hope in hell of diverting me from the path my character has chosen. I've had plenty of arguments over certain heavy scenes, particularly the ones involving violence in my Mak Vanderwall series, but I trust that my characters know what is best and therefore stand by my writing.

The book is boss and the characters know. I am the

creator and the slave to them. My successes are my own, as are my failures.

I abhor routine and as a result I don't have any typical working day, except perhaps when I am on hard deadline. On those days I wake, turn off my phone, get a coffee, turn on my laptop and work solidly until I hit my word count or until the day ends, with only short breaks to eat and stretch. It is physically unhealthy to sit and stare at a computer for twelve to fourteen hours a day so I don't like to work like that more often than needed. There have been a lot of deadlines lately, mind you. As I write this, I am wearing anti-glare glasses and wrist splints for carpal tunnel earned from writing two novels back-to-back.

I am a big believer in accuracy and I will do almost anything—short of murder—to get the researchable elements of a story right. Research. Research. Research. The crime genre requires it. Many readers think that my main character, Mak, is autobiographical and that my *real* father must be the formidable Detective Inspector Les Vanderwall. I'm sorry to disappoint you. My father sold fridges and stoves at a department store and I had barely met a cop until I started researching the crime series.

For the past fifteen years I have immersed myself in criminal cases, investigation, criminal psychology, psychopathy and the study of homicide and violent crime. I have toured the FBI academy at Quantico, shot guns with the LAPD, taken polygraph tests, researched with world expert on psychopaths, Dr Robert Hare, seen autopsies, spent time in morgues, in squad cars and with private investigators and homicide squads. I've been set on fire by stunt company West FX and earned my Certificate III in private investigation at the Australian Security Academy.

When Mak was choked unconscious by an assassin in *Siren*, I felt I needed to experience that, so I arranged for ultimate fighter 'Big' John McCarthy to show me how it felt to black out from oxygen deprivation. The sensation was intense and surprising, and there is no doubt in my mind that I couldn't have written that scene correctly unless I had experienced it myself.

Hands-on research is how I get inspired.

MY RULES

I am wary of writing tips.

Some of my favourite authors disagree passionately on how to write and what traps should be avoided or tools should be banned (for example, exclamation marks, adverbs, italics, internal dialogue, etc.).

My writing tips, if you must know them, essentially boil down to one five-letter word: WRITE.

The only way to be a writer is to write.

There is no other way. No amount of discussion or theory can make you a writer. The only way to write is to write. In the words of Gertrude Stein, 'To write is to write is to write is to write is to write is to write is to write is to write.'

The act of writing is always a risk. It's taking a chance. The trick is to not let uncertainty or procrastination defeat you. Don't think you need to write as others have. Don't make yourself believe you need to make every word perfect as you set it on the page. The act of writing is still the best way to learn how to write. Writing is individual. In the end you need to trust your own instincts and just dive in. Do it. Let the words take you. Let the story be the boss.

FIVE MUST-READS

1. **On Writing** by Stephen King: Part writing manual, part autobiography, this is a must-read for any aspiring novelist.

2. **The Handmaid's Tale** by Margaret Atwood: A near-future dystopia with terrifying parallels with real-life extremism.

3. **The Road** by Cormac McCarthy: A wonderful exercise in the beauty of darkness.

4. **The diaries of Anais Nin**: A raw and fascinating look into the life of a brilliant and original woman.

5. **Dracula** by Bram Stoker: Love it or hate it, this remains one of the most influential, copied and frequently adapted novels of all time. It must be read.

TAKE A LITTLE TIME FOR THE COUNTRY TO KNOW YOU

by Adrian Hyland

My initiation into the life of crime began—like many others before me—somewhere out in the badlands west of Alice Springs. I had been in the Territory for a couple of years and done a stretch in the usual professions open to your Melbourne University Arts graduate (shovelling shit on a drilling rig and driving a truck) before landing a job in 'Aboriginal community development', a rather loose description which left open the obvious question, who was developing whom?

Looked at through the lens of time, it was an amazing occupation for a writer. For weeks at a time I'd go cruising around the desert, helping people return to places they'd walked out of 30 years before. It was late October. The weather was hot, but not lethal (that would come later). There were maybe twenty of us in four Toyotas. By day we'd roam the mulga and Spinifex plains, digging out old soaks, patching tyres, dispatching the odd marsupial. At night we'd eat, drink, tell stories and read books—those of us who could.

I'd yet to shake the dust of uni from my boots, and was rather, er, *precious* about my reading (if it hadn't been written by a dead white Oxbridge male, forget it). Somewhere among the billies and bones in the back of the Troopie you would have found battered volumes of Coleridge, Byron, Celan, Tsvetayeva and Kerouac (well, okay, they weren't all Oxbridge, and they weren't all male, but you get the picture).

Among the other whitefellas travelling with me was a bloke named Toly Sowenko. One night Toly pulled out a novel and began reading it by the campfire light, chuckling as the story took hold. I asked what was so funny and he read out a few paragraphs. Intrigued, I took over the book when he fell asleep, and encountered, for the first time, phrases like 'she gave him a look that ought to have stuck four inches out of his back'. What I discovered was writing that was better than much of what I'd read at uni and a social critique as deliberate and deeply felt as those of Orwell or Steinbeck.

The writer, of course, was Raymond Chandler, and it was somewhere on that trip that the thought first occurred to me that maybe crime fiction could be an appropriate vehicle for satisfying the hunger simmering in my brain.

Also on the trip was a young woman who shall remain nameless but who, after a hundred permutations and what feels like as many years, would emerge as Emily Tempest, the protagonist of *Diamond Dove*.

From time to time, I cop criticism from those who consider it inappropriate that a middle-aged whitefella should write about a young black woman. This never comes from Aboriginal people; those who've read the books tend to find them amusing. It comes from well-meaning lefty types who believe that Indigenous Australians should be left to tell their own stories.

There's nothing I love more, of course, than seeing Aboriginal people telling their own stories. Indeed, I worked for years in Indigenous education trying to help them do just that. I think of Alexis Wright's *Carpentaria* as one of the most significant works of our age. But I do have a problem with these armchair critics, most of whom would die of thirst if they ventured beyond pedalling distance of their inner-city terraces, telling me what to write. Bugger them. I'm doing what authors have always done: engaging with the world around me, imagining other people's lives.

I spent ten years in those communities, and had the privilege of living with people that barely exist anymore—old men and women who had grown to adulthood before they ever made contact with whitefellas; the last of the nomads, quite literally. These people amazed me then. They amaze me now. They remain the touchstone by which I've judged humanity ever since, and much of what I've written has been in tribute to them.

An incident springs to mind: another Tanami bush-bash, another group of elders. After a long hard day, we sat by the fire yakking and sipping tea. Too much tea, I realised at two in the morning when I woke up in need of a piss. I took my torch, staggered down to the creek bed, groggy, and was swiftly rendered un-groggy when a massive king brown reared up and struck out at me. I gaped in horror, dropped the torch, and scuttled back to camp.

'You right there, Jupurla?' one of the old men asked.

'Bloody big snake down there.'

He followed my gaze, nodded, casually remarked: 'Don't you worry. Take a little time for the country to know you.'

I thought about this as I drifted off to sleep. *Take a little time for the country to know you?* It's the direct opposite of how a whitefella would have put it. There was enough going on in that sentence—the idea of a snake as the voice of a landscape, of country knowing people—to fill a dozen novels.

This conflict—the collision between this nomadic culture and the threshing machine of Western technology —is the most significant engagement being fought in the country today, and yet it is almost completely absent from our literature. I wanted to change that. If I had a goal in writing, it was to bring that struggle to a wider audience.

Why did I end up choosing crime? The genre seems a natural fit for the outback, particularly the rough mining town in which I often found myself. The place was riddled with criminals and fraught with violence. Many Aboriginal people were reacting angrily to the stresses of deracination, and many whitefellas thought of it as a place to hide. I'd been up there for about a year when it occurred to me that I knew seven people who'd done time for homicides of one kind or another. I'd come across drug-runners, gun-runners, a serial killer and a Russell Street bomber. (In Victoria, the closest I'd come to the underworld was a friend who'd been convicted of damaging a Marlboro billboard.)

Rough mining towns are an excellent grounding place for a crime writer—for any sort of writer, in fact. The thing about big cities is that you tend to settle somewhere comfortable and stay put. The danger in this is that your literary creations may owe more to books than to real life (Joyce Carol Oates, come on down!). In a small town, you get up close and personal to the sort of people you'd rarely see in the city, and you're forced to accommodate them. Even among those who didn't have criminal records, there were some seriously weird people.

This is how I described the town in *Diamond Dove*:

> *A bigger collection of dickheads and drop-kicks you'd have to travel a long way to find: boozers, bruisers and substance-abusers, rockjaw Germans and lockjaw Yorkshiremen, grease monkeys and gamblers, meat-workers, meat-heads, missionaries, maniacs, men on the run, men on the dole, men on the Witness Protection Program. Peddlers, pushers, whores and bores, desperadoes of every denomination. You name it, they were there, drawn to the town like flies to a carcass.*

Perhaps what I most value about the crime novel is that it has a defined structure, and I am a person who needs structure. My earliest literary efforts were monstrous, amorphous things. I showed one once to an assessor who said: 'You write well enough, but where's the structure?'

She had a point: the thing was bigger than *Moby Dick*, but the craftsmanship was more Enid Blyton. So I reworked it into a crime novel: bumped off a few characters, sprinkled in a few clues and a dash of sex, wrote a flashy denouement, and there you were. It went from a blob in the bottom of the drawer to a saleable item.

I also value the crime genre because it's such a broad church. I'm still extremely eclectic in my tastes—my inspirations range from Phantom comics to Chinese poetry—and I figured any genre that can embrace writers as diverse as Reginald Hill, Dorothy Porter, G.K. Chesterton and Kinky Friedman could surely find room for yours truly.

The best advice to the aspiring writer I've come across is in Haruki Murakami's *What I Talk About When I Talk About Running*. This ninja of the imagination writes novels and runs marathons, and regards each as training for the other. What running and writing share is a need for effort and desperation, for focus and ferocity.

Don't waste your time doing courses, reading how-to books (well, except for this one) and dreaming about downing pastis in Les Deux Magots and swapping bons mots with Stephen Fry. Get off your backside and write. Turn on the computer, get out the pencil (don't laugh— I seem to work at about the same speed, whether I'm using the laptop or the pencil—Shakespeare churned 'em out with a feather) and dive in.

My insights into the mechanics of the writing process are few and far between, probably of not much interest to anybody but myself. But here are a few of them:

1. Character

Character is the heart and soul of the modern novel, and crime seems to be better at creating it than any other branch of the trade. Think Miss Smilla, Sherlock Holmes, Philip Marlowe, the elusive Father Brown. These people are alive. We know them, love them.

My favourite character in crime fiction is the great Andy Dalziel, he of the omnivorous appetites and sledgehammer humour (and cursed be the BBC for stripping away that gargantuan personality and squeezing it into a gimcrack television series). When Reginald Hill died a while ago, I felt as if I'd lost a friend. Not Reg: Andy.

I personally find that I can't create characters out of thin air, and I'm wary of characters 'borrowed' from other works of art (or worse—the bloody telly). I need a real person to begin with. They might be heavily disguised, dressed up, stripped down, gender realigned, but somewhere in there lurks a living, breathing human being.

In my second book, *Gunshot Road*, I introduced into the narrative a slightly crazed young woman.

'You had one of those in your first book,' commented my editor, Mandy Brett. 'You can't have another one. You'll start getting stereotyped—the feller who does the crazy ladies . . .'

The trouble was that I needed an unbalanced character to propel the plot forward at one or two vital moments.

'Maybe you could just change her to a male?' Mandy suggested.

So that was what I tried to do. But it didn't work. The new character just wouldn't come to life. I dicked around with him for weeks, scribbling page after lousy page. Then, one afternoon, I was out splitting wood, when a memory rose to the surface: a troubled youth I'd known, drink and drug-addled, destroying a radio with his nulla nulla.

Zap! That was it; I had my man. I pulled out a notebook, did a quick character sketch, saw at once how to fit him into the story. I achieved more in those five minutes than I had in weeks (I also wonder, in retrospect, whether the adrenaline or whatever you get from heavy physical activity didn't have something to do with freeing up the imagination).

2. Get rhythm

My publisher, Text, has an annual award known as the Text Prize for Young Adult and Children's Writing. This seems to me to be about the toughest nut to crack; the experts tell you write about what you know, and childhood is the one thing everybody thinks they know. Consequently, there are thousands of manuscripts cruising around the slush piles at any given moment.

Dropping into the office one time, I glanced at the daunting pile in the corner of the office and asked Mandy: 'How the hell do you work your way through that lot?' The answer—depressing for any writer—was that most of them get no more than a few minutes' consideration. A page or two, maybe a chapter, is often enough to gauge the quality of the work.

'So what's your criterion for quality?'

'The rhythm of the language,' she replied. 'If your author's got a tin ear, you can tell straightaway. Whereas if they can write a decent sentence, chances are they can write a paragraph; if they can write a paragraph . . .'

So there you have it—or at least one esteemed editor's view of it. It's all about rhythm.

And how do you enhance the rhythm of your language?

There are lots of tricks, but for me the most important is to read your work out loud; say it 'slowly and deliberately', as I once heard the Clancy Brothers declaim. Listen to the way the consonants clash, the vowels harmonise.

Your writing should do more than tell a story or describe a character; it should *reflect* the story, manifest the character. It may be my imagination, but it seems to me that writers of a Celtic background—Ken Bruen, Chris Brookmyre, our own dear Shane Maloney—are the masters of this art. I suspect there's a dash of Celtic poetry—filtered through Joyce, Dylan Thomas and Hugh MacDiarmid—circulating in their blood.

3. Read. Widely.

This may sound like a quote from Captain Obvious, but when I teach writing, I'm always astonished by the number of young wannabes who have written more than they've read. Is it television? I don't know, but unless you look like Elle Macpherson (who famously commented that she didn't read books unless she'd written them) you're not going to get away with that.

Your writing is a reflection of your reading. If your reading isn't up to scratch, there's a pretty good chance your writing won't be either.

4. Revise, and then revise some more

I'm a revision Nazi. I never stop; if I had my way, I'd be creeping around the bookshops, pencil in hand, making alterations to my books. I tend to pour it all out in the first drafts, and then get out the scalpel and cut the flab, scrap the bits a reader will skip. To me, the goal of revision is concision. This applies both on the micro and the macro levels—from each sentence to the whole book.

I remember once trying to describe the scene as Emily Tempest steps into an outback bar. I became a little obsessed with light and its illimitable manifestations. I even read Newton's *Opticks*. I rambled on for pages, describing sunbeams refracting off bottles, bubbles running down amber glass, the glimmer of gristle snagged on an old man's tooth. When I paused for a cup of tea, I picked up Patrick White's *Riders in the Chariot* and came across a sentence in which he described the drawing room in a country homestead: 'It was difficult to tell where the light ended and the glass began.' I remember putting the book aside with a soft sigh, mourning the fact that I would never have the imagination to crash two images together like that.

Peter Temple does this all the time. His novels are like haiku written by the Seven Samurai. The best writers are like that. They are alchemists; they take disparate elements and refine them into gold.

5. My last piece of advice

Ignore all advice, mine and everybody else's. Forge your own path, which is what every other decent writer has done.

Many writers surround themselves with good-luck charms or trinkets, mementoes, quotes, photos of their favourite authors: things to inspire them. I'm no exception. Taped to the piano next to my desk is a picture of the Chinese dissident Liu Xiaobo, who is currently serving an eleven-year stretch in a Liaoning prison. His crime? Doing what writers do: writing.

I spent a winter once in Liaoning. Just being in that icy wind-swept province was tough enough; what it would be like in a prison there, God only knows. Think frozen gruel, fingers blue, frostbitten toes . . .

Liu is about my age and has spent his entire professional life banging his head against the brick wall of Chinese authoritarianism. His *entire* life. Imagine the determination you'd need to do that, to confront the juggernaut. Chinese people are brought up to respect the state and are expected to conform. In writing as he has, Liu has gone against the grain, rejecting everything he's been raised into. And for what? For something as slippery and elusive as a notion of freedom.

Banging your head against a brick wall seems to me a pretty good analogy for what we do as writers. We in Australia may not live in a corrupt dictatorship, but we're all seeking freedom of a kind: freedom from illusion and deceit, freedom to imagine.

Whenever we pick up the pen, we become players in a great tradition, that of questioning, criticising, shining a spotlight into the darker corners. There are dark corners aplenty in this wide brown land of ours. I'm not much of a believer in evil, but I do see us as divided (more by nurture than nature) into two opposing camps: those whose primary concern is for their fellow creatures, and those whose primary concern is for themselves. The latter camp, of course, is our bête noire, and I see it everywhere: in the guise of the paedophile priest, the oleaginous journo, the self-satisfied businessman; sometimes it will squeeze into a fluoro jacket, jump on the back of a mining truck and bellow: 'Axe the tax!'

Whenever it rears its ugly head, it's our duty to confront it. And crime, more than any other genre, seems willing and able to carry out this job. That's what they're all doing, all the great detectives: Marlowe, Challis, the unsinkable Cliff Hardy, the bumbling Murray Whelan.

As I write these lines, I'm floundering around in the dark waters of a new novel. I've got very little idea of what it's going to look like. It's an amorphous mass—or mess. I'm not even sure what genre it's going to be. All I see is a handful of images: a blind woman caught in a bushfire, a galloping horse, an orchid with a flame-shaped labellum. And some words of Yeats that keep rolling through my head:

> *The threefold terror of love, a fallen flare*
> *Through the hollow of an ear;*
> *Wings beating about the room;*
> *The terror of all terrors that I bore*
> *The Heavens in my womb.*

Somehow, I have to weave these scattered fragments into a coherent narrative. From down here in the foothills, the peaks look insurmountable. The way the world is going—and I write—the publishing industry will have collapsed before I finish the bloody thing.

This is where Liu Xiaobo comes in. If things look tough from where I am, I try to imagine what it must look like from a prison cell in Liaoning.

All you can do is start. Write something. Anything: a sentence, a paragraph, an episode. Keep chipping away. Interrogate the memories. Imagine those you can't find. Attack every sentence as if it were the slab of ice beneath which a loved one was frozen.

If things go okay, maybe something worthwhile may emerge, a book that will be on the shelves for about the life span of an ant. A delaying action against the inevitable darkness. A kick against the pricks.

Not much, perhaps, but about the best we can hope for.

SIX MUST-READS

1. **The Last of the Just** by André Schwarz-Bart (a forgotten masterpiece).

2. **The Collected Songs of Cold Mountain** (the Red Pine translation, if you've let your Chinese slip).

3. **Miss Smilla's Feeling for Snow** by Peter Høeg (darkly magnificent central character more than makes up for a confusing plot).

4. **On Beulah Height** by Reginald Hill (as brilliant as the above, but leavened with the presence of Andy Dalziel).

5. **For Esme—With Love and Squalor** by J.D. Salinger (the perfect short story).

6. **And for a nightcap, try: The Lantern out of Doors** by Gerard Manley Hopkins.

Adrian Hyland is the award-winning author of the Emily Tempest novels, Diamond Dove *and* Gunshot Road, *along with the acclaimed* Kingslake-350, *an intimate look at the Black Saturday bushfires in Victoria. He lives in north-east Melbourne and teaches at LaTrobe University.*

MAD, BAD AND DANGEROUS TO KNOW

by Leah Giarratano

The very first presentation I gave at a writers festival was entitled, 'Mad, Bad and Dangerous to Know'. No, the organisers weren't trying to sum up my bubbly personality; they wanted a panel of crime writers to discuss what makes a fictional villain different to a real criminal.

One of the other writers felt that the Hannibal Lector–style villain had become a cliché, a figure based more on fantasy than reality. He argued that baddies in crime novels should be more like criminals in real life—normal people who make bad choices and find themselves on the wrong side of the law. I listened with interest and didn't interrupt even though I disagreed.

Hannibal Lector may well have been the figment of Thomas Harris's imagination when he wrote *Silence of the Lambs*, but that doesn't mean that people like him don't exist. I know because I've met some of his real-life peers.

I had always wanted to meet a psychopath . . . until I did. I'll take you into the experience. Imagine, for a moment, that we're walking into one of the most secure units in New South Wales corrections. My first visit was as part of my clinical psychology doctoral degree when I was studying severe personality disorders. The unit is intended for patients who are extremely suicidal or who self-mutilate, but because it's high security, it often houses inmates who would be murdered if they were held with the main prison population.

You can sit in on an interview with one of these men.

Wait! Before we start, we should listen to the supervisor—a psychologist who's seen it all. For some reason, he warns us *not* to read the inmate's file before the interview. This has never happened to me before.

'You're not allowed to do an assessment on this one,' he explains. 'I don't want you to even speak.'

The door opens. The room is quite small. There are no windows. Two chairs. A desk. Soon there are seven people inside, including the jail hierarchy—people I've never seen in this unit before. Uniforms. It's standing-room only for you and me. I'm up against the wall, near the door. Sitting in front of us, on one of the chairs, my supervisor has his back to us. In the chair opposite is a small guy with a full beard and a shiny, black, bruised eye.

Suddenly, I know who he is—one of the most despised men in Australia. We're meeting him today because when his wife left him he abducted their young children on an access visit and murdered them. He kept the little girl alive for a couple of days, and I'm not going to tell you what he did to her. That's why we're not allowed to read the file.

Later my supervisor explains that this killer has been separated from the main prison population for security reasons. The people gathered in the small room must decide whether it's safe for him to serve his sentence in the main jail. And if he wants to stay in the unit, he has to convince them that he's in danger. To do that, he has to apply for forensic status—claiming that he was insane at the time of the murders and is horrified by what he did.

Trouble is, he just can't do it! This man is a true psychopath. He doesn't feel remorse for what he did to his children. Quite the opposite—he's proud of it. Other prisoners commit pathetic little crimes, but he's the real deal and he can't keep his sense of superiority from his face or voice.

This man is not unique. I have met other monsters just like him, never exactly the same, but with enough chilling similarities to make them extremely dangerous. The neighbouring unit is less secure and the inmates have access to therapies like art and group counselling. I visited one day when I wasn't wearing my contact lenses and I missed an important sign stuck up on the officers' wall.

Blithely, I spent a good deal of time studying the paintings of one man, who I'll call Bobby X. The paintings looked pretty good and Bobby seemed to enjoy leaning over them with me, standing close together. It was only later, when I returned to the guards' room, that I noticed the weird looks the guards were giving me. That's when I glanced at the sign above the door.

> *Warning to all female staff.*
> *Do not come into close contact with Bobby X.*
> *He bites.*

A female officer had lost part of her ear when she'd strayed too close to Bobby. And previously, his victims had been tied up with dog chains, raped and bitten.

I'm not telling you these things to shock or to prove that monsters exist outside of fiction. I'm trying to explain why I write the books I write.

I have been a clinical psychologist for seventeen years, specialising in treating psychological trauma. One of my first patients was a Vietnam veteran who had lived for decades with terrible memories of his mate being shot in the head. I treated him using a technique called exposure therapy, which involves the patient speaking about the traumatic event over and over, unpacking every detail, examining every sense and feeling—thoughts, smells, sounds, images, somatic sensations—until the terrible events become a cohesive, integrated narrative. It becomes a normal memory—always distressing, but not continually intruding unbidden into the consciousness.

By the end of our treatment sessions, for the first time since the war, my Vietnam veteran slept without nightmares full of blood and brain matter, and he didn't have to spend his days half drunk to get rid of the dreadful images.

I was hooked. Pretty soon I was working in a psych hospital on a unit set up specifically to treat traumatised veterans. Our reputation grew and before long we were dealing with civilian heroes—police, fire and ambulance officers—as well as victims of armed robberies, terrible car accidents, rape, muggings, kidnappings and pretty much every hideous thing you can imagine.

I became fascinated with all aspects of trauma, including the effects of abuse on children. Some grow up to live happy, productive lives. Others develop one or more of a range of psychiatric problems, including post-traumatic stress disorder, depression and substance-abuse issues. Sadly, a very, very small number of abused children absorb all of the violence inflicted upon them and fantasise about the day they will be able to inflict it upon others.

Becoming a writer

People ask me when I first knew I was going to write novels, and I guess I've known since I was in third grade. Yet it wasn't until much later that I decided exactly *what* I wanted to write. After one particularly bad day at work, I came home and wrote the first scene of *Vodka Doesn't Freeze*, almost vomiting the words onto the page. Unwittingly, I discovered my very own exposure therapy, learning how to process the terrible things I encountered by turning them into stories.

Towards the end of my jail placement I met a prisoner with a particular paraphilia called picquerism. This sexual disorder is common to sexual sadists who have an obsession with stabbing, usually others, but who may also ritually stab themselves. Jack the Ripper was a picquerist. So was serial killer Albert Fish, who had more than two dozen needles inserted into his groin, which were revealed by an X-ray after his capture. My particular picquerist began to whisper to me in my dreams until I wrote my second book, *Voodoo Doll*, which featured a psychopath nicknamed Cutter.

Exposure therapy and writing involve almost the same process: examining a scene from every single angle, exploring the emotions, unpacking the details. Many of the things that I imagine don't end up on the page, but they must be considered, studied, picked up and put down again. And then there's the editing, reading the work over and over, deleting here, adding there, deleting it all once more. Just as the shattered bytes of data are refashioned in the traumatised patient's brain, the writer's imagination and memories are also plundered to create a new tale.

And for me, the writing process provides a similar level of relief from the build-up of years of painful therapy sessions. All of the baddies who've hurt my clients go in my books and then I punish them! They get bashed up, shot up or locked up (sometimes all three). And by the time I'd written the third and fourth novels, *Black Ice* and *Watch the World Burn*, I was finally calm enough to write in the genre I'd always wanted to: young adult and urban fantasy.

My latest series—a trilogy called *Disharmony*—still contains a psychopath and plenty of violence, but it won't be traumatising young minds or filling the pages with poison.

How did I get published?

The first thing you should take from this section is this: 'Don't try to get published the way I did.' The second thing you should take away is this: 'Maybe you should.'

They say it never happens—an unsolicited manuscript from an unrepresented author being pulled by a publisher from a 'slush pile'. Well, it happened to me—and not by just one publisher . . . by four. By the time I heard back from the agents I'd approached I already had a two-book deal with Random House following a minor bidding war.

Naturally, I told the agents thanks but no thanks!

I'm still unrepresented—by choice. I've done every deal without an agent, and have a new three-book deal with Penguin. The way I see it now is that when I sign with an agent I want them to be someone who can really do a lot more for me than I can do for myself. I won't just sign with anyone now. I have my eye on a select few, but they hardly ever sign new authors. Attracting their attention is a major mission for me.

In the meantime, some publishing houses are big enough to have rights departments and can act as agents once you're signed. They take the book overseas to book fairs and are dedicated to trying to sell the book to the widest audience possible. Many authors would disagree with my strategy, arguing that having an agent is essential. And to be honest, it is very difficult to attract the attention of a publisher without one—although most publishing houses in Australia now accept unsolicited manuscripts with caveats. It is worth checking their websites to see the latest guidelines on submissions. Make sure if you're afforded one of these golden opportunities that you submit *exactly* the way they ask you to, and direct the submission to the right person. And cross your fingers! It might just happen.

Creating compelling characters

I suspect it might be the same for most writers, but getting to know and love my characters is my favourite part of writing. I guess it comes easily to me, probably because of my psychology background. I know how and why people will think and behave given most situations—even extremely stressful and distressing situations—so worrying about realistic reactions doesn't really happen for me.

As to plotting, however . . . well, just shut up. Gah! Plotting's hard.

But we're talking characters . . .

Inner conflict

Compelling characters are not perfect heroes or unstoppable villains—they all have flaws, vices, insecurities and quirks. The best characters have inner conflict that compels them to make mistakes, to stumble and bumble into dangerous waters, to miss opportunities and ruin their chances to succeed. Why would we care about a character who gets it right all the time? Struggle is more compelling than languid satisfaction. Struggle creates tension and if you don't know this by now you should probably go out and get a new tattoo: *tension is everything*. Our characters need to change and grow, suffer and learn something about themselves. They need conflicting sides to their nature—parts of their character that are not easily reconciled.

The most interesting characters have sides to them that they don't know about, or at least, that they don't *want* to know about. And it's even better if we, the reader, can see these personality traits.

I'll share a psychology strategy with you. It's called 'the Johari Window' (Luft & Ingham, 1950) and it's a great way to map out the inner conflict that drives your character. The window states that we have four different parts to our selves.

	Known to self	Not known to self
Known to others	**Open Self** (what you openly show the public)	**Blind Self** (what you are not aware of but others might know)
Not known to others	**Hidden Self** (what you do your best to keep hidden from others)	**Unknown Self** (parts of your nature that no-one knows—not even you)

Using this model you can create and explore the hidden depths of your characters and give them authenticity in their motives and reactions.

The Open Self is obvious: these are the traits that your character (and the reader) is aware of.

The Hidden Self holds the parts of your character's

nature that they prefer to keep hidden—beliefs, attitudes and attributes that your character is aware of but prefers to not show the world.

The Blind Self contains the parts of your character that you (as the author) are aware of, but your character is not. It can be interesting to show your reader these aspects through action and dialogue while your character is blithely unaware of them.

The last quadrant is the most mysterious of all. *The Unknown Self* includes traits that the character and the reader are not aware of. We only learn to recognise these facets of ourselves when we have a sudden realisation or a change of heart about something we didn't know we felt strongly about.

Map these four aspects of personality and you will see ways your characters can grow and change through the story. Each quadrant of the window is likely to be a different size. For instance, if you have a particularly duplicitous character in your book, they would have a large Hidden Self, full of attributes and attitudes they try to keep secret from the world. A very forthright, trustable character (a mentor-figure, perhaps) may have a large Open Self, but you could plant a small Hidden part to their personality, which makes them more interesting. A flawed protagonist would likely have a large Blind and Unknown Self that could change as they develop during the story.

Strength and energy

Wimps suck. They're boring. Even if our characters are flawed, dark, broken in some way, they must have strength to be compelling—for us to care what happens to them. We don't just read to see ourselves—we read to see ourselves as we could be. Sacrifice is strength and all great heroes make sacrifices—the willingness to give up something of great value. Your character may be a super-hero, serial killer or a servo-attendant, but they should be bigger than their circumstances. Great characters act—they don't sit around waiting for things to happen.

Loving the bad guy

All of us have a dark side. When writing your baddies it helps if you can find your own. If you can have empathy for even your most sadistic killer, your reader will not be able to tear their eyes from them.

Bad Men Do What Good Men Dream: this is the title of a book on my shelves, written by forensic psychiatrist Robert I. Simon. Simon argues that all of us have the capacity to commit terrible acts, but societal norms keep our primitive, sometimes 'evil', desires in check. A number of social science experiments have shown us that given the right (or maybe that should be wrong) circumstances, normal people will do terrible things.

Take the Stanford prison experiment. A group of uni students were enlisted to participate, selected specifically because they had no criminal or adverse psychological history, and were assigned randomly to be either a prisoner or a prison guard. Philip Zimbardo, the head researcher, simulated a prison environment, giving the students uniforms (including batons and reflective sunglasses for the 'guards', with the 'prisoners' stripped of their names and assigned numbers). The experiment ran 24/7 but had to be shut down six days into its planned two-week run when a third of the 'guards' were found to have exhibited sadistic tendencies and the 'prisoners' were becoming terribly traumatised or dangerously angry.

Stanley Milgram conducted an equally famous experiment, having also recruited uni students. They were asked to participate in a study about the effects of punishment upon learning. Three people were in the room: the student and two confederates—one dressed in a lab coat, the other strapped to a machine, which purportedly administered electric shocks. The student was given a sample of the 'shock' the 'learner' would receive, so that they would think the whole thing was real.

The learners were asked to read items aloud. When they got one wrong they received a shock. With each mistake, the student was asked to increase the 'voltage'. There were 30 levers, each corresponding to fifteen volts. If a student hesitated they were told, 'The experiment requires that you go on.' Meanwhile, pre-recorded yelps and then screams could be heard through the partition separating student and learner. When the highest possible voltage was administered there was silence from the other room.

Before the experiment, a poll was taken of a separate group of students, explaining the set-up, and asking them what percentage of students they thought would continue right up to the 450 volt range (the max). The poll estimated that 1.2 per cent would be prepared to inflict the maximum voltage. In fact, 65 per cent of students went right through to the conclusion of the experiment. They carried on turning up the voltage until the screams died.

Milgram interviewed the volunteers afterwards, asking them why, and was told they were just following orders. Does that sound familiar? It's the same excuse offered down the ages. The man in the white coat or the military uniform is seen as a legitimate authority figure. Someone to be believed. Someone to be obeyed.

When writing a villain we don't necessarily have to completely get in touch with our shadow selves, but we do have to be curious about why people do terrible things. Think about the nature–nurture debate. If you were raised under different circumstances is it possible you could be antisocial?

We also need to think about why so many of us like to be deliciously terrified reading about these monsters. Why are we sometimes compelled to look at car wrecks?

What is attractive about being frightened? Can frightening people be attractive? These questions are important because they help us to understand our villains.

One-dimensional characters are flat, have a single motivation and are easy to pigeonhole and ignore. Create a rich, detailed, compelling baddie by examining their life from many different angles. Villains should have complex motives and act in ways that surprise us. Some baddies are the most attractive character in the story. They have cleverness and charm. They can have the best lines. They are powerful and resourceful, which increases not only the stakes, but also the menace and suspense.

Most baddies are not *all* bad, even if their actions are completely unforgiveable. We can be repelled and drawn to our dark characters at the same time. As their creator, we must get inside their skin, care about them, love them even when they're truly heinous.

If you can love your villain, you can love this genre.

References

Luft, J. & Ingham, H. (1950), 'The Johari window, a graphic model of interpersonal awareness', *Proceedings of the Western Training Laboratory in Group Development* (Los Angeles: UCLA).

Simon, R.I. (1996), *Bad Men Do What Good Men Dream: A forensic psychiatrist illuminates the darker side of human behavior* (Washington: American Psychiatric Press Inc).

MY RULES

1. Everyone has a book in them, or likes to think so.

In the end, most will assign this dream to their bucket list, along with salutes to the sun in Tibet with the Dalai Lama and tequila shots at Lake Como with Leonardo DiCaprio and George Clooney. If you want to be published it will take more than a positive affirmation in front of the mirror. You're gonna have to work for this.

2. Don't listen to your inner critic.

If you're terribly lucky this inner voice will tell you: 'You can do it! Go for gold!' Much more likely, it will whisper that you're not quite good enough; you're ugly and fat; everyone else knows the meaning of life, how-freaken-lame-are-you? Murder your inner critic. Drown them in a bathtub or strangle them. If they're dreadfully persistent, I prefer a fork for stabbing. It's so much more satisfying.

3. Are you sure you want to do this?

Everyone better than you has already written everything important. Why would you want to have a go? How are you at all relevant in the world? (You've not quite assassinated your inner critic, have you? Sulphuric acid is a perfectly legitimate aid to dissolving a body. I believe you can get it on eBay.)

4. So you still want to write a book.

Well, ideally, you should be a gifted writer, and not only because your mummy said, but because unrelated others have told you so repeatedly. Now the hard work begins. Write. It will take longer than you think, especially when real life keeps interrupting. Write the whole thing. (Why should any agent or publisher care about an outline from an unknown person?) Then, if you dare, read everything the agents and publishers say about your novel. I know it's a little like offering your arterial veins to a vampire, but blood must normally be given. So arrange your lily-white neck and press 'Send'.

5. Are you interesting?

Lucky you! The media has a microsecond attention span, and should your personal story not ramp up the Sexometer or provide an instant 'hook', you could face some obstacles getting publicity. Unless, of course, your words are so fabulous that what you write outweighs how marketable you are.

6. Should you blog and tweet?

I know the online world can break a book before the publishers even know what the hell happened. I also know that authors can become so obsessed with their online presence that they fail to actually produce words on a page. Sometimes forums and tweets should be murdered. (See earlier reference to sulphuric acid.)

7. Write what you know and research well.

If you've had access to a specialised world most don't get to see, write about it. If you haven't, do your research thoroughly. If there's a fire in one of my books I access specialist fire investigation texts and thoroughly digest the details. Sometimes I only use a single line of that research, but it still makes a difference. Who cares if you don't use everything you learn? Readers will appreciate your efforts and you'll be smarter in the long run. Win-win.

8. Learn to improve your visualisation skills.

When beginning my writing day, I close my eyes and breathe, shutting out the rest of the world. I try to leave where I am behind me and dive into the world I am writing about. If I'm a psychopath, plotting my next kill, I want to know what I'm seeing and how I'm feeling. What does it smell like? What does the setting do to my subconscious? Maybe I'll use none of these details in the book, but it is great to be here, inside your character, breathing the air that she does.

9. Listen to your editor even when it hurts.

The first few times it feels like a personal attack, no matter how nice they are, but you're part of a team and they're the experts in what they do.

10. Keep reading.

I go through periods when I am too busy to read and my writing suffers as a result. Carry a book (or your e-reader) everywhere you go.

11. Good luck!

I really hope to buy your book at an airport one day, or maybe we'll meet at a writers festival and I'll ask you to sign it for me!

FIVE MUST-READS

1. The Raw Shark Texts *by Steven Hall: Very strange! A story about dissociation, amnesia and love. But read quickly; the story is literally devoured by a metaphysical shark even as you scurry through the pages.*

2. The Man Who Mistook His Wife for a Hat *by Oliver Sacks: Think a nonfiction book about neurological disorders could possibly be the most fascinating thing you'll read all year? You'd be right.*

3. Bad Men Do What Good Men Dream: A forensic psychiatrist illuminates the darker side of human behavior *by Robert I. Simon: Another nonfiction text, equally fascinating, but do read with the lights on. And a torch. And at midday.*

4. The Lord of the Rings *by J.R.R. Tolkien: I think it's actually illegal to have not read this book. And if you're thinking of breaking the law, you're depriving yourself of one of the most delicious journeys ever.*

5. Vodka Doesn't Freeze *by Leah Giarratano: Hey. It's my list! Read it because the title's so cool. Or read it because it was an unsolicited, unrepresented manuscript that created a minor bidding war between four publishers.*

Dr Leah Giarratano *is a clinical psychologist and author of four crime fiction novels, including* Black ice, Voodoo Doll *and* Vodka Doesn't Freeze. *Her current novel is* Disharmony: The Telling, *the first of a trilogy. She has also hosted the TV documentary series* Beyond the Darklands, *in which she delved into the psyches of some of Australia's most feared criminals.*

THE SECRET FORMULA

by Michael Robotham

I have spent a lifetime trying to understand the writing process. I have folders bulging with interviews and profiles of famous writers—everyone from Graham Greene to Samuel Beckett—describing their writing process. I thought that I could learn from these masters. If my desk faced the right way (avoiding the view) and if I started work at the right hour (6 a.m.) and if I had just the right amount of coffee and alcohol and mistresses, I too could produce a great novel.

As a result of this research, I have a wealth of trivia about writers. I know that Lewis Carroll wrote all his books standing up and Henrik Ibsen, the Norwegian playwright, had a picture of his arch rival pinned over his desk to spur him on. Voltaire got rid of boring guests by pretending to faint. Jonathan Swift didn't talk to

anyone for an entire year. Raymond Chandler said he
was inspired to write by watching his wife doing house-
hold chores while naked. (I did suggest this to my wife
and have the bruises to prove it.)

Having written eight novels (and ghostwritten
fifteen 'autobiographies'), I am no closer to understanding the mysterious art. Each practitioner discovers their
own formula. We confront the tyranny of the blank
page and find a way to triumph over our doubts and
fears.

Some writers find it easy. Linwood Barclay once
told me that he could 'dash a novel off in three months'.
R.J. Ellory said it took him about six weeks, while
Alexander McCall Smith regularly writes 10 000 words
a day. I envy their output, but save my anger for those
writers who claim to agonise over every single word,
polishing a sentence a day, or taking long walks to
ponder each paragraph. Shakespeare wrote 37 plays and
154 sonnets, averaging 1.5 plays a year, as well as raising
a family and running an acting company and theatre.

I'm not a fast writer, but I'm prolific. I work long
hours. I write because there's nothing else I want to do.
It's my job, my hobby, my life.

I can pinpoint when it began. I was eight years old
when I discovered a storeroom at St Stanislaus Catholic
Primary School in Gundagai, where the nuns kept
blank exercise books, pens, pencils and erasers, which
were handed out as required. I loved the smell of that

cupboard. I loved how everything was new. One day I sneaked into the classroom and stole a blank exercise book, tucking it in the waistband of my shorts beneath my shirt.

There was something about the blank pages that fascinated me—the pristine white surface, the smell of bleached paper, the faint lines that ran horizontally across each page. I would sit for hours contemplating what to write. A diary? An adventure? Poetry? Lists? Sadly, no matter what I chose to write, my words didn't match the magic of the moment. The instant I put pen to paper, I had spoiled the pristine pages. I ripped them out. Began again. The result was always the same.

As a teenager—I can't remember the exact year—I discovered the short stories of Ray Bradbury, the wonderful science fiction writer. I remember reading the opening of *The Illustrated Man*, wide-eyed with wonder, as two strangers shared a campfire and one unbuttoned his shirt to reveal dozens of tattoos. In the flickering firelight, the ink-drawn images began to breathe and move, each telling a story.

I went looking for more of Bradbury's work, finding *The Martian Chronicles*, *The Small Assassin* and his most famous novel, *Fahrenheit 451*, about a future totalitarian state where books are banned and burned. Then I struck a problem. In my small town, I couldn't get any more of Bradbury's books. They weren't available. I made a decision. I wrote a letter to 1221 Avenue of the

Americas, New York, because that was the address on the flyleaf of one of his books.

Months passed. I didn't expect to hear anything back. Then a parcel arrived at the post office. My mother had to collect it. I came home from school and it was sitting on the kitchen table, wrapped in brown paper and tied with string. Inside there were five books—the Ray Bradbury titles that I couldn't get in Australia—as well as a letter from the man himself, saying how thrilled he was to have such a passionate young reader on the far side of the world. It was an astonishing gesture—life-defining if not life-changing. Almost from that moment, I wanted to be a writer.

I had one major difficulty. My small-town upbringing and idyllic childhood had equipped me to write about small towns and idyllic childhoods. I didn't have Ray Bradbury's imagination and I felt that Mark Twain had stolen the best plots when it came to fishing holes and swimming holes and cooking up a mess 'o catfish for cousin Emmy Lou. I needed material. I needed to live a little and explore the big emotions. Deferring a place at Sydney University to study Law, I applied for a newspaper cadetship and started my career with another future Australian writer, Geraldine Brooks.

I thought journalism would be a perfect career for a would-be novelist and in one sense I was right. What other profession allows you to interview presidents, prime ministers, pop stars and psychopaths (and that's just the p's)? What other job can take you deep into the bowels of the Moscow State Archives to uncover the Rasputin files and the diaries and letters of the doomed Romanovs?

However, I soon came to understand that most creative careers are a conspiracy *against* writing, because there is only so much energy to go around. Every waking moment I spent chasing the next story or making contacts. I didn't have the spare time or the creative vigour to write a novel. It might've been better if I'd chosen to be a postman or a cobbler or a maker of widgets.

I didn't seriously attempt to write a novel until I was 33. My wife was pregnant with our first child and we were living in London with a mortgage in negative equity. Our respective parents thought I was crazy and selfish. By then I had a wealth of material to draw upon, but all the bravado and confidence of youth had evaporated. Who was I kidding? What made me think I could really write?

I tried. I have a book called *God's Waiting Room* sitting in my bottom drawer. It is not a crime novel, but it does have a mystery. Set in a small fishing town in Australia, it attracted an agent and a UK publisher, but fell at the final hurdle. 'It was too Australian,' I was told—which sounded more like an excuse than a valid reason.

Putting the novel away, I took a detour and became a ghostwriter. It seemed like a logical step. Having spent my career writing pieces that were rarely more than 800 words long, I questioned whether I had the patience, stamina and perseverance to spend a year on the same project. Could I work on my own? Could I capture someone else's unique voice, the colour and drama of their life, and bring it to the page?

I ghosted fifteen autobiographies, for politicians, pop stars, soldiers, adventurers and actors. Twelve of them were *Sunday Times* bestsellers, but my name was never mentioned on a book jacket and often not acknowledged. This never bothered me. The people who counted—publishers and agents—knew my work.

I was writing full time and making a good living, but the desire to write a novel never left me. In 2001, in between working with Rolf Harris and Lulu, I wrote 117 pages of a book that became *The Suspect*. I didn't know it was a crime novel. I didn't know how it ended. I sent it to my agent with no higher hopes than getting it published, selling a dozen copies (bought by my mother) and putting it on my own bookshelf. Then I could say, 'Hey, I did it!'

It didn't happen quite like that. The part-manuscript became the subject of a bidding war at the London Book Fair in 2002 and was eventually translated into 22 languages. Every dream I had ever had of being a novelist came true in a hectic few hours of deals being done in the back of black cabs and figures scrawled on serviettes. I was euphoric. Amazed. Stunned. Then came the terror. What did I know about finishing a novel? I was unknown and untested, with no idea how my book ended or what it was about.

The Suspect turned out to be a Hitchcockian-style tale of a man who finds himself in the wrong place at the wrong time. I chose a psychologist as my main character because I've always been fascinated with human behaviour; and I gave Joe O'Loughlin early onset Parkinson's because I thought there was a tragic irony in having a protagonist with a brilliant mind and a crumbling body.

Up until I wrote *The Suspect* I had read very few crime novels. I was misquoted in my very first newspaper interview, which carried the headline: *The Crime Writer Who Has Read Only One Crime Novel.* I had explained to the interviewer that I tried to read 'one of each' of the major crime writers, but this got misconstrued. The quote has followed me around the world as interviewers ask, 'Which one?' They assume it must have been the *worst* crime novel in the world or the *best* one—why else would I have stopped at one?

Don't get me wrong—I love the crime genre. Some of the finest writers in the world work exclusively in the genre or dabble in it periodically; authors like Peter Temple, James Lee Burke, George Pelecanos, John le Carré and Daniel Woodrell.

I hate this perpetual debate about genre fiction versus literary fiction. It bores me. Literary snobs are as foolish as those genre writers who feel aggrieved at not being long-listed for major prizes. (In particular I'm thinking of the *New York Times* bestselling crime writer who famously and fatuously claimed he could write a Booker

Prize–winning novel in a fortnight if he set his mind to it.) Why make the comparison? A great literary novel can change your life and resonate through the ages. A great crime novel can shine a light upon the best and worst of human nature and into the darkest corners of society. They are what they are. The writing process is the same. It still requires putting one paragraph ahead of another. Isolation. Imagination. Loneliness. Despair.

Early in my career I agreed to teach a few writing workshops. I was embarrassed. Most of the attendees knew more about writing than I did. Some of them were professional workshop attendees and I wanted to tell them to stop wasting their money. Teaching writing is like telling someone how to ride a pushbike. You can instruct them to sit up straight and pedal like crazy, but until they climb onto a bike they can never understand the hundreds of tiny adjustments to steering and balance and speed. Writing is exactly like this. I can't teach somebody when to break into dialogue or when to use an adjective or, more importantly, when to *stop* using them. This is about gut instinct and experience and trial and error. But when it feels right, the words will create sentences and the sentences will become paragraphs and the paragraphs will quicken and develop a heartbeat. You are creating a monster. It lives, it breathes, it thinks, it consumes you . . .

There is a mystery to creative writing but it's a boring one unless you're interested in the minutiae of finding the right word. Ernest Hemingway rewrote the last page of *Farewell to Arms* 39 times. An interviewer asked him: 'Was there some technical problem? What was it that stumped you?'

'Getting the words right,' said Hemingway.

Knowing the process by which novels are written won't keep many readers turning the pages. It's like that famous Otto von Bismarck comment on the legislative process: 'Laws are like sausages—you sleep far better the less you know how they are made.' And the so-called 'writing life' portrayed in movies—the drinking, bedding awestruck post-grad students and avoiding crazed fans with sledgehammers—is another myth I'm afraid. Basically, I sit on my arse all day and wrestle with words that refuse to come easily.

Sure there are basic rules. And every one of them has been broken or bent or turned on its head by writers who are brilliant enough to pull it off. Even the most basic of them such as, 'show don't tell' and 'make your protagonist likeable', are not so much rules as suggestions. The only one I have ever seen that holds true in every great novel (as well as film, TV and on stage) is the necessity of having memorable characters. They don't have to be saints. They can be rogues, chauvinists, serial killers or conmen, but they must be compelling. The deeper and richer the character the more emotion you can put into them and the more your story will come to life.

233

Your character must always want something, and something or someone must stand in their way. It may be love or a better job or to solve the crime or to win the girl. Conflict is what sets up a story. How a character meets these challenges. And despite what you may read elsewhere—it is 80 per cent about character. That's what brings readers back to a writer years after they've forgotten the plot of their favourite novel. It's the characters they fall in love with. It's the characters they care about. It's the characters you nurture as a writer.

Some writers are pioneers and others are settlers. Some charge forward, planting flags as they go so they can find their way back later. Others build towns and set up shop, not moving on until they're happy. I think I'm a settler. I write a strong first draft, rewriting as I go. I do not plan ahead. I rarely have any idea how a book is going to end until I'm almost finished. I figure if I don't see it coming, neither will the reader. If it surprises me, it should surprise them. Not everyone can write this way, but that doesn't make it good or bad. As I mentioned at the very beginning, there is no secret formula.

George Orwell said, 'Writing a novel is like having a long illness.' William Faulkner said it was 'like a one-armed man trying to nail together a chicken coop in a hurricane'. Dean Koontz said it was 'like making love, but it's also like having a tooth pulled. Pleasure and pain. Sometimes it's like making love *while* having a tooth pulled.' John Irving said it was 'like tossing your parachute from a plane and jumping out after it. You have to believe that you'll somehow be able to grab hold of the thing before you hit the ground.' Ernest Hemingway said, 'There is nothing to writing. All you do is sit down at a typewriter and bleed.'

I don't know about the shedding of blood. Writing is hard, but it's not boxing or brain surgery. For most people it begins as a hobby and like all passionate hobbies it must become an obsession. Don't write for the money. Write because you love it. Write because it helps you make sense of the world. Write because you can't go a day without it. Write because you are compelled to write, because you don't have a choice and if they outlawed it tomorrow you would be scribbling by torchlight in the basement as the jackboots marched through the streets above.

Forget about formulaic plots, clichés, stock characters and standard-issue dialogue. Things have changed. It won't work anymore. It shouldn't work. There are too many good writers struggling to get published for someone to emerge who doesn't deserve the privilege. The quality of the writing, the depth of the characterisation, the originality of plotting, the breadth of knowledge on display, all of these things are genuinely breathtaking in some modern crime novels. Not in all of them, but the best of the best.

Finally, I am going to leave it to the master, Stephen King, to describe the writer's life. Mr King has been very generous about my work—which is another reason I will sit in my rocking chair in my dotage and feel satisfied. King writes:

> *There is indeed a half-wild beast that lives in the thickets of each writer's imagination. It gorges on a half-cooked stew of suppositions, superstitions and half-finished stories. It's drawn by the stink of the image-making stills writers paint in their heads. The place one calls one's study or writing room is really no more than a clearing in the woods where one trains the beast (insofar as it can be trained) to come. One doesn't call it; that doesn't work. One just goes there and picks up the handiest writing implement (or turns it on) and then waits . . .*[1]

At the beginning of this essay I mentioned another one of my heroes, Ray Bradbury, and I should now add a postscript. The great man was once quoted as saying: 'Jules Verne was my father. H.G. Wells was my wise uncle. Poe was the bat-winged cousin we kept in the attic. Flash Gordon and Buck Rogers were my brothers. And Mary Shelley was my mother. There you have my ancestry.'

Last year I wrote a story about Bradbury's generosity to me and I described him as my literary father while Steinbeck and Hemingway were my over-achieving older brothers. A few weeks later I received an email from Bradbury's daughter, Alexandra. I had no idea that Ray was still alive, in his nineties, living in California.

She wrote: 'I just finished reading your article to my dear old dad and he asked if I could contact you and let you know that he thought your piece was wonderful. He cried when I read it to him and then exclaimed that you were his honorary son.'

If that doesn't make it worthwhile—nothing else will.

Endnotes
[1] This passage was published in the essay, 'The Writing Life', *Washington Post*, 1 October 2006.

MY RULES

1. Don't forget the character arc!

In every story, the key character is irreversibly changed for better or worse.

2. A good character has to endure both internal and external conflict.

Your character must always WANT something and something must stand in their way.

3. Every paragraph should do one of three things:

- *Provide essential information*
- *Move the story along*
- Define character.

4. Characters should each have their own voice.

5. Great dialogue only 'sounds' real.

The dialogue used by good writers is stylised and unexpected. It is shorter, snappier and funnier than in real life. Characters don't always say what they're thinking.

6. Good fiction begins with story and progresses to theme.

It almost never begins with theme and progresses to story.

7. Write, write and when you're sick of writing, write some more.

It's the only way you get better. And then read. The books that inspire me to write are those that are less than perfect. I take them apart, see what works and doesn't work before deciding how they could have been better. Then there are the books that are so beautiful and seamless, I cannot see how to take them apart or begin to understand how they were put together. They lift my spirits but bruise my heart because I know I'll never be that good.

FIVE MUST-READS

1. A Moveable Feast by Ernest Hemingway: I was 22 years old when I first read Ernest Hemingway's posthumous memoir about his early days as an unknown writer in Paris. Three years later, I carried a battered copy of the book with me when I visited Paris for the first time. I sat in the same cafés and walked the same streets.
I still have my original copy of the book, now patched, yellowed and dog-eared. Whenever I pick it up, I cannot shake the urge to write. I can picture myself in Paris, ordering a half-carafe of white wine and a dozen oysters before sharpening my pencils and opening my blue-backed notebook. I may never write a word to match that of Hemingway, but I can live the dream and strive to write one true sentence, the truest sentence that I can.

2. A Prayer for Owen Meany by John Irving: 'I am doomed to remember a boy with a wrecked voice—not because of his voice, or because he was the smallest person I ever knew, or even because he was the instrument of my mother's death, but because he is the reason I believe in God; I am a Christian because of Owen Meany.' This is the opening line. How could anyone not read on?

3. Miss Smilla's Feeling for Snow by Peter Høeg: Long before Lisbeth Salander, Harry Hole and Kurt Wallander emerged from the snows of Scandinavia, another giant stepped from the ice. Her name was Smilla Qaavigaaq Jaspersen, but she's best known as 'Miss Smilla', a heroine with an unforgettable voice and a feeling for snow.

4. A Secret History by Donna Tartt: A truly great literary thriller.

5. The Broken Shore by Peter Temple: A modern Australian classic.

Michael Robotham is one of Australia's most popular and widely read crime writers, his books having been translated into 22 languages. He is a twice winner of the Ned Kelly Awards for Best Crime Fiction and a perennial bridesmaid in many other international awards. You can read more about him at www.michaelrobotham.com.

THE ART OF SUSPENSE

by Katherine Howell

I've always wanted to be a writer. As a child I used to make tiny books out of folded paper and scribble a picture on each page. Later I copied out poems I liked, and wrote stories of my own—usually about girls whose parents bought them a pony (a dream of mine between the ages of eight and twelve that sadly never came true).

In my teens I produced Trixie Belden fan-fiction for my schoolfriends, then became obsessed with Stephen King and tried to write horror. I found I was great with the gore but crap with everything else, and it suddenly seemed that perhaps I wouldn't have a novel published before I was twenty. In fact, it took until I was 37. It wasn't horror, either, but crime—though still with the gore, as I took my fifteen years' experience as a paramedic and put it on the page for fictional paramedics and detectives to struggle through.

I write a book a year now. Even if I wasn't contracted or published, this would still be so. I write because it's who I am. It's how I sort out what I think and how I feel. I keep a diary alongside each novel I write, and every day before I start work I sit down and blather away, writing about where I'm up to in the book, what I think might happen next (or that I have no idea), and what else is going on in my life. It's amazing how often I solve story problems by rambling on about various possible solutions.

I can look back at the diaries of previous books and see, for example, that I always feel this disheartened at the halfway point, full of doubts about whether I can pull off the ending. I used to imagine that writing would get easier with experience, or that eventually the fear of failure would vanish. It never does. But this is actually reassuring because it means I've felt this way before and survived. I can do it again.

Frantic was the first novel of mine to be published, but actually the fourth that I'd written. The first three are stashed in a cupboard, and the only time they see the light of day is when I need a page for a 'what not to do' demonstration in a writing workshop. People often ask me if I think those manuscripts can be resurrected, if I can now tell what's wrong with them and how to fix them. The answer is yes, I *can* tell what's wrong, and that's precisely why they'll never come out of the cupboard.

The first one was about a cult, and in the end every character was dead. The second one was a Patricia Cornwell imitation, with the rider that because I knew next to nothing about forensic science I made my protagonist a first-year student who also knew nothing. The third was a crime story about cops chasing a murderer, but because I struggled to find out how police solved their cases, I brought in a ghost as a helpful sidekick who could magically produce a clue whenever I hit a dead-end in the plot.

All these ideas are fatally flawed: killing everyone in the cult is a cliché, hiding a lack of knowledge behind a new student is lazy, while using a ghost to solve your crimes is just plain silly. These novels don't deserve to be salvaged. I spent so many years (around twelve, all up) writing and rewriting the manuscripts that they carry what I call the 'stink of despair'. I only have to read a paragraph to immediately relive the feelings of frustration and dissatisfaction that accompanied them. When I compared early attempts with published works, I could recognise that something was lacking in mine, but I didn't know what it was.

My wonderful agent gave me encouragement through each improved draft and writer friends would tell me that I was getting closer. Finally, I began again and wrote a different novel—this one about a female paramedic whose baby is kidnapped. My agent liked the idea but said the novel didn't work because there was no suspense. How could there be no suspense? The BABY is KIDNAPPED, for goodness sake. I sat down and re-read the draft. She was spot on. The manuscript was boring. I didn't care about the characters I'd created. My heart didn't race for them. Why?

By then I had started a Masters degree in writing and decided to research suspense for my thesis. What is it, exactly? How does it work, and how can a writer develop it? My ulterior motive was clear. If I found the answers, I might be able to rescue my novel.

I threw myself into my research and learned first of all that suspense is necessary in all narratives, crime or otherwise, because that feeling of tension and curiosity is key to keeping the reader reading. Then I learned that there are two crucial elements: first, readers need to care about the characters, and second, readers need to feel uncertain about what's going to happen to those characters.

In that early draft of my novel, the main character is paramedic Sophie, mother to ten-month-old Lachlan and wife to police officer Chris. The story begins with Sophie at work one night, called to a body hauled out of a river. She's shocked and horrified to find that the dead man is her husband. Chris was supposed to be at home with Lachlan, but Sophie's desperate search fails to find the baby. The investigating police believe that

Chris committed suicide and took the baby with him as he leapt into the water. Sophie doesn't know what to believe and for some time into the narrative I portrayed her as completely frozen by grief and doubt, because I believed this was how a real person would behave in such a situation, and I felt readers would recognise that and be able to identify with her. I was wrong.

Sophie's passive response meant that she didn't drive the narrative action forward at all, and instead was dragged along by the events like a bag of wet sand, holding back the story's pace and momentum. In addition, because half the story was being told from inside Sophie's head, it was unrelentingly grim. Readers of crime thrillers want to be entertained, not depressed.

The other point of view was that of the baby's kidnapper, and in those sections I showed that he not only felt bad about what he'd done, but was thinking about giving the baby back. This lessened the tension instead of ratcheting up the suspense.

The reader didn't really care about Sophie, because she was so static and negative, and when I made it clear the baby wasn't in mortal danger, the reader had nothing to be concerned about anymore. The only remaining scrap of uncertainty in the novel was the identity of the kidnapper, but in writing from only two points of view, I had pretty much answered that as well.

I started again. This time I drew on further research into techniques and methods to initiate then build suspense. Three years later, I posted the all-new manuscript back to my agent. This time she said it worked, and took it to publishers Pan Macmillan. I knew that if they liked it, their next question would be, 'What else do you have?' so I'd also sent along a one-page outline of the next book in the series I was already imagining. A month or so later, my agent rang and told me I had a two-book deal. It's a dream moment in any writer's life, and to celebrate it I burst into tears.

And here I am, seven years later, with six books on the shelf and two more under contract. Paramedic Sophie appears now and again, but the main character of the series is Detective Ella Marconi, and each book has her working on a new case in which paramedics become entangled. I use a kind of rotating cast of characters for the paramedics and also the police officers who work with Ella. Sometimes a character who appears in the background of one book will have a major role in the next, or vice versa. And I take care to show in later books, even in a small way, what's happened to these characters (usually regarding their relationships).

When I sit down to start a new book I don't outline the story. I devise the starting situation—who will die and why, how to involve the paramedics, what direction Ella's investigation will initially take—then I begin to write. I don't have detailed profiles of characters, just enough details to let them loose on the page.

Writing is usually hard, though there are occasional marvellous days when the words flow and it feels like I'm watching a film where the story just unfolds in front of me. I aim to write around 2000 words a day once I get past the first couple of chapters, and often this becomes a matter of telling myself to 'Just write 500 words. Write that much then you can have a break. Five hundred is nothing! Any fool can write 500!' I usually find that once I get that far I'm on a roll and can keep going. Some days it's harder again, and I have to say to myself, 'Just write 250!' Whatever gets the words on the page is a good system.

My writing day is not particularly organised. My most productive times tend to be in the afternoon, so I often use the mornings for emailing, writing workshop notes and whatever else needs to be done. This changes when the deadline draws closer and everything else in my life gets a little neglected (sorry, honey).

I research as I go, though I sometimes do a little beforehand if there are things I need to know for the opening scenes. I tend to learn much more than I ever use because I've learned that research is like a garnish: you just need a little bit to make everything right. Too much clogs the pace and too little leaves the story bland.

In those early struggles, for example, I felt the need to write the paramedic's jobs exactly as they happened in real life, so if we had a person trapped in a car crash, and we took their blood pressure ten times, that's what I put on the page. That meant of course that my paramedic scenes went on interminably. I came to realise over a number of drafts, and by analysing what published authors put in their books, that I needed enough information to colour the scene but not so much that it slowed down the story. As a writing teacher once told me, 'Starting a story is like putting the reader on a roller-coaster. Too much detail is like stopping them part-way and asking them to look at the lovely ornamental shrub over there. They don't care—they want to get on with the ride.' (Thanks, Veny Armanno.)

I have a year to write each book, and at the end of that year I send it to my publisher, editor and agent. They all read it, and the publisher and editor then get together and discuss it before writing me a report. This is generally around ten pages long, and the first half-page usually says how much they love it while the next nine pages go into detail about the problems.

There are always problems: a writer is too close to see how well the different elements are working, so the editor and publisher play an essential role in the production of a book. I haven't written any that weren't crime, but it seems to me that this is especially true in this genre, where I'm trying to hide clues and the truth about the killer, but can't see how well I'm doing because I already know the answers. For example, in one book

I'd mentioned a certain clue three times, and thought they might ask me to add it in once or even twice more. Instead the editor told me I'd referred to it too often. If I hadn't had that input, I would most likely have added the clue again and blind Freddy would have picked the ending way too early.

When I get that report back I feel flat for a couple of days, because even though, as I said, there are always problems, in some small dim-witted corner of my heart I had hoped the manuscript would be the most perfect they had ever seen. Overcoming my disappointment, I set about solving the problems and giving the story more emotional impact, while increasing the tension and suspense. For the next six to eight weeks I become a recluse as I try to make all these great ideas a reality.

The reworked manuscript goes back to the editor and publisher, who read it again. Each time (so far) I've received a big tick of approval. There is still time to make changes. The novel has to pass through a copyeditor who looks for smaller issues: style, word and phrase repetition, inconsistencies in names/places/times/descriptions/facts, etc. Then the manuscript comes back to me, and I read it again and make further changes (tightening paragraphs and polishing sentences).

This process of re-reading and rewriting continues even after the novel is typeset into page proofs. By now, I'm certain it's the most boring pile of tripe in the world. I've read the best lines so often they don't seem fresh or brilliant anymore. But again, my diaries tell me that I always feel this way.

The first time I saw *Frantic* in a bookshop felt so strange, almost like I'd made this book in my bedroom and sneaked it onto the shelves. It doesn't feel that way now, but I can never see my books in the same way I see anyone else's. I imagine this is how a parent feels when looking at their small child surrounded by others in a playground. You can't see its strengths and weaknesses clearly. You can't say for sure how it compares.

Waiting for the first reviews can be excruciating. Every author I know wants each book they write to be better than the last, but how can you tell? There are so many elements to a book, so many things to juggle, plus so much going on in your life and mind as you write. You as the author have changed. You are not the same person who wrote the previous book. You're older, perhaps wiser. You might be happier, sadder or struggling to cope. In the end, all you can do is rise to the challenge and keep writing.

I consider myself so fortunate to be able to write and publish books. I still get a tremendous kick out of hearing from readers who stayed up all night or missed their bus stop or forgot to feed their kids because they were so engrossed. But mostly I love the power of words.

When I was a kid I used to lie on my bed and be

transported to the blizzards of the American mid-west by Laura Ingalls Wilder, ride along sunny British lanes with Jill and her pony, and creep through creaky buildings with my old pal Trixie. I love that now I get to create similar worlds for other people; that a story from my imagination gets transmitted to yours; that I can make you laugh and cry, make your heart race and your palms sweat, make you fall through the page and into the world that I've created.

MY RULES

1. **Read, and not just in your genre.**
   Read anything and everything.

2. **Pull apart the books you love most and try to work out how the author is making you feel what you're feeling.**
   Get to recognise and understand the frame that holds the book together.

3. **Use all the senses in your writing.**
   It's easy to get caught up in what a character sees and hears and forget the other senses, but smell especially can be powerful.

4. **Don't give up just because it's hard.**
   It's hard for everyone.

5. **Invest in yourself, with both time and money.**
   Do some courses. Pay a reputable mentor. Listen to feedback that comes from people who know, not just your family and friends who a) love you and b) might not be sure how to explain what doesn't work.

6. Don't be frozen by the blank page.

Five hundred crappy words are better than no words at all: at least you can come back later and fix them.

7. Readers want to feel something and be entertained.

It's your job to produce writing that does that.

8. The more you rewrite, the better your work will be.

9. Keep a diary and pour out all your concerns and worries about your writing there, then close it and get on with the work.

10. Writers write.

Enough with dreaming about doing it: sit yourself down and begin.

FIVE MUST-READS

1. **Bitterroot** by James Lee Burke

2. **Madame Bovary** by Gustave Flaubert

3. **Paris Trout** by Pete Dexter

4. **Dark Places** by Kate Grenville

5. **Valley of Grace** by Marion Halligan

Katherine Howell is the author of the bestselling series featuring Detective Ella Marconi, which includes Frantic, Cold Justice *and her latest,* Web of Deceit. *She is published in multiple languages and is the only author to have twice won the Davitt Award for Best Crime Fiction, for* Frantic *and* Cold Justice.

You can read more about Katherine on her website, www.katherinehowell.com.

GITMO HERE I COME

by Lindy Cameron

A few years ago I needed to blow something up (several somethings actually). One seemed pretty obvious—a US Consulate—but the others less so: a train, some helicopters and a high-rise carpark. I also needed to shoot a few people, but we'll start with the bombs.

Once upon a time (back in LBI—Life Before Internet) researching how to make an explosive device was rather hit and miss. Sources for a good bomb recipe would have been: a library or university; a demolition expert, clearance diver, explosives specialist or chemistry professor; or my Great Uncle Eugene who used to build elaborate rafts to blow up on his dam—just for fun.

Since my recipe required untraceable-back-to-me materials, I sensibly decided to leave Uncle Eugene out of the evidence chain and rely on the help—conscious or otherwise—of the aforementioned demolition or ammo experts. The usual MO for this kind of nefarious plot is to get the expert drunk at a pub (local to his army base or copper/uranium mine), spike his drink, finagle him into a compromising position and blackmail him into aiding and abetting. Either that or I could steal his keys, slip into his place of work and carry away all the ingredients before he regains consciousness.

Next I would have to make the bomb, plant it, detonate it, rejoice maniacally in my awesome powers of destruction—before realising too late that I had left some kind of 'trace evidence' behind, which would soon see me cornered in my lair and either sent to prison or, more likely, blown sky-high in an accidental or self-inflicted blaze of glory.

So many books, TV shows and movies have used this scenario that my advice would be: *Don't use it, ever. Put—the drunken—bomb specialist—down—now!*

Having said that, an inventive (or re-inventive) writer can walk right up to a plot cliché and twist it into a brilliant *tour de force* that no-one has ever read. Most plot devices have been used before. What really matters is what happens in the 300 pages *after* the set-up. Will the villain detonate his extra big bomb? Will the heroes cut the right-coloured wire at T-minus three very sweaty seconds?

Ideas come from the strangest places so it's probably

a good thing that writers spend so much time on their own—away from people who think their ideas are weird, or worry they're contagious, or believe their own lives are fodder. There is always the chance, of course, that our weird concepts are born and bred by the very solitary nature of our existence. Either way, it's really only other writers who understand when a fellow scribe poses a question on Facebook like: 'How long does it take a 115-kg man to exsanguinate?' And 'Does anyone know of a lethal poison that could be applied via the "normal" use of toilet paper?' Or 'How do you knock out a satellite when you don't have your own guided missile (yet)?'

My need to blow up the various things was triggered by the type of book I was writing—an international action thriller. In the process of writing *Redback*, my world-domination plot morphed and detoured because my research dragged me down bifurcating paths— kicking and screaming with glee.

At one point, a Discovery Channel documentary on Apache helicopters engendered a small obsession. Did you know that the Apache AH-64D and the Apache Longbow are put together like a meccano set by ordinary people like you and me? By that I mean seriously ordinary, un-mechanical, is-this-a-spanner-or-a-wrench type of people. Ten or so helicopters get assembled at once, in a huge hangar, by teams of men and women in overalls each assigned a set task, like fitting the seats, or putting in the electrical cabling, or riveting the whatsits to the hoojahs. These teams don't move from station to station; instead the whole helicopter is pushed by human power into the next bay where the 'rivet team' or the 'cockpit team' go to work. So, these things arrive as a chunky metal skeleton and get transformed into Hunter-Killer flying machines, armed with Hellfires, Sidewinders and other 'folding-fin rockets', as well as 1200 rounds of ammo for the 30mm Chain Cannon.

I fell in love with these Apaches, which was why I knew that I had to find a reason to blow one up.

Redback was inspired by many things, mostly unrelated to my research. First, I had a desire to write something a little different from my regular PI mysteries. Second, I was motivated by sheer anger at the shock-and-awe assault on a certain country that *we* all knew had no WMDs. And third, I wanted to experience the joyous *woo-hoo* feeling of blowing shit up! Yes, I know, this is wrong on so many levels, but I'm a writer and sometimes it's my job to point out why we *shouldn't* blow things up . . . by blowing things up.

The bomb I used for the US Consulate in Peshawar didn't need any specs. It was just a bomb. It went *kablooey* and caused a LOT of destruction. The train bomb was the same—although I had need of techy words like 'detonating device'.

The carpark bomb was a different matter. Because of its 'home-grown terrorist' angle, I wanted to make a fertiliser bomb of the kind Timothy McVeigh used in Oklahoma. My primary research tool was the Internet, which I trawled for stories about homemade bombs and blowing stuff up. This is when I began to expect the FBI, CIA or US Homeland Security would send a special request to ASIO, demanding to see my file.

Digressing here for a moment, I am in some respects an Internet Pioneer of the Literary Kind. (Genre fiction only, so don't be alarmed.) Way back in 1997 when the Internet was a geeky invention, and dial-up connection speeds were slower than stampeding turtles, I was commissioned by the Museum of Victoria to write a murder mystery to promote an international conference. My story was going to be serialised 'On The Internet' one chapter a month for ten months.

Google didn't really exist in 1997. It was simply a research project started by two Stanford University PhD students. And although the 'information superhighway' was a familiar catchphrase, there wasn't really much accessible or useful stuff *on* the Internet—for crime writers anyway.

My cliff-hanging, monthly serial adventure was called *Stolen Property* and was set in Melbourne, Cairo and Peru. One of the few sources of information was the local library where I had to borrow actual reference books and read about these places. I also had to make phone calls to people who might know things. For a crime novel that was being showcased on the geekiest thing then in existence, the research was decidedly 'old-school'.

Stolen Property was free to online readers (of which there weren't many), but since I was being paid to write the adventure serial, I can daringly lay claim to being perhaps the first crime author to make money from the Internet.

My brand-new publisher at the time was about to release my first PI novel and decided to get in quick and publish the newly titled *Golden Relic* as a paperback to coincide with the last chapter of *Stolen Property* being posted on the Internet, and in time for the launch of the museum conference. Just over a decade later, after being out of print for five years (although the twelve-dollar paperback had been reselling on eBay for $90 to $300!) that same book, my debut novel, has returned home to the Internet, entering the twenty-first century as an ebook.

This brings my digression full-circle because the Internet has become the most powerful tool at any writer's fingertips, while at the same time providing scientific proof of the existence of the WPG (writers' procrastination gene). No other invention in human history has saved (and wasted) so much time. The www is a *very* dangerous thing for the unwary writer. There is so much more 'everything' at our beck and call—facts and figures, truth and lies, history and current affairs.

One of the great traps for writers is to fall in love

with their research and bore readers witless with reams of *stuff*. It doesn't matter how interested I became in Apache Longbow helicopters, my job was to remain focused on writing a page-turning thriller with action heroes, bad guys, guns, bombs, katanas, terrorist plots and brave rescues. There's only so much techno-babble a reader can take before you simply have to blow that sucker to smithereens.

The greatest menace to page-turning, fast-paced fiction is the author who forgets to leave 80 per cent of their research in a shoebox under their bed. The writer who doesn't understand that 'less is more' will simply irritate readers rather than impress them. On the other hand, if you can weave some awesome details into the middle of a running gun battle while also using whip-smart dialogue, then it's clearly an urge that must be obeyed.

This again brings me back to the Internet as a price-less investigative tool. My Googling had already given me access to: the Apache specs; explosive devices; info on model planes; and lots of facts about all kinds of Australian, UK and US government departments, agencies, forts and seats of power.

Even so, for a short while, I assumed that I'd have to use my special writer's licence to invent the place where I was going to carry out two of my acts of explosive carnage. In my mind I pictured the first blast in a multi-storey carpark in 'downtown USA' somewhere, while the second bomb had to detonate in a place an Apache helicopter might visit.

All hail Google Maps! Randomly scrolling across satellite maps in the relevant US state, I spotted a perfectly situated military base. I zoomed. I toggled. I gazed in utter amazement at how much the map showed me. Quite sensibly, large chunks of the base were blurred— but I had more than enough for my purposes. I could see the surrounding roads, right up to the main gates and then inside. I could see the buildings and parade grounds and manicured lawns. I zoomed in again. I spied tarmacs and hangars . . . and something else: helicopters.

Zoom to maximum: Apache helicopters. *Be still my beating heart.*

Who knew the US cavalry now rode choppers? (*Thumping Ride of the Valkyries/'napalm in the morning' aside.*)

Even better, barely 250 kilometres away, there was a large city with a multi-storey parking station just waiting to be blown up. I had my location. I had my targets. I didn't have to invent things. (You can't make this stuff up—even when you try.) I studied the maps and prepared my plot, picturing where I would plant the bombs . . .

Wait! Was that a sound outside? Cocking my head, I stared out of the window. In that instant, I imagined men in camo-gear and night-vision goggles crashing through my windows and bashing down the doors. I would be hooded and spirited off to Gitmo, or Germany or Dubbo, or some other clandestine place of rendition and torture.

I told myself I was being paranoid. I laughed it off. That was until six months later when I woke to the news that Homeland Security had arrested a terror cell on US soil that had allegedly been using Google Maps to plan an attack on a major commercial airport.

Truth and fiction aren't strangers at all. Which just goes to show that there are dangers inherent in any kind of research—from paper cuts to being placed on an FBI watch list.

MY RULES

1. Writers procrastinate—just accept it.

You can, however, use your procrastination to your advantage. So, don't bake a pavlova, bathe the dog, give the galah a manicure. Read, research or write instead. (And yes, of course you can avoid writing by writing.)

2. Read instead of painting the back fence.

You should be doing this anyway. A writer who doesn't read—a lot and widely—probably only thinks they want to be a writer. (I could suggest a host of great Aussie crime novels and thrillers, but then I'd be procrastinating on your behalf.)

3. Research instead of replanting the pittosporum . . . again.

While research is not, technically, a form of procrastination, going on the hunt for stuff you might need for a book you may write next can be quite therapeutic; and rarely a waste of time.

If you need some good research excuses, try these topics: hunter-killer helicopters; warrior women; sniper rifles; gravity wells.

Yes, they're my topics, but they're really good ones. (Drop me an email with any good links you find.)

4. Write something else instead of watching Dr Who.

Blogging about your last or current or next book might not increase your WIP (work in progress) word count, but at least you're thinking about your book, and you are writing.

Reviewing some great Aussie crime/thrillers to help raise all our profiles is also a good use of your 'other writing' time. At least you're helping, and it justifies all that reading. (Correction: Watching Dr Who is never a form of procrastination.)

FIVE MUST-READS

1. **Five Go to Smuggler's Top** by Enid Blyton
2. **Biggles Flies South** by W.E. Johns
3. **From Russia with Love** by Ian Fleming
4. **By the Rivers of Babylon** by Nelson DeMille
5. **The Wire in the Blood** by Val McDermid

---

*Publisher and author **Lindy Cameron** has written the action thriller* Redback, *the* Kit O'Malley PI *trilogy, and the mystery* Golden Relic. *She is also co-author of the true crime anthologies* Killer in the Family *and* Women Who Kill. *Lindy is a founding member and National Co-Convenor of Sisters in Crime Australia, and publisher of Clan Destine Press.*
www.clandestinepress.com.au

A WRITING LIFE

by Gabrielle Lord

If you want to be a writer, it's probably best to start early. My writing life began before I went to school, listening to my mother read to me, slowly absorbing the words. I don't even remember when I *learned* to read, it seemed to be something I could always do, and I still recall the delight I took in kindergarten reading a story called *The Little Fir Tree*. That little tree, sometimes green, sometimes covered with snow, ended up as the Christmas tree in a home, decked with candles and baubles. There was also a story concerning a rock pool and the creatures that lived within it.

In those days it seemed to me that the world and everything in it was so much *closer* to me than now. I could look at those pictures and somehow *be* in them, with that little fir tree covered in snow, or crouching over the translucent water, looking at a starfish in the rock pool.

Not all illustrations I encountered in kindergarten were happy. Every week, Mother Declan turned the pages of a large wall chart and one of those pages showed a portrait of Lucifer—a massive, terrifying black-and-green demon with bat wings, fiery red eyes and fangs, torturing poor souls struggling in an eternal sea of flames, their arms raised in useless supplication. Another chart picture showed a sentimental pink-and-white angel, hovering behind a pair of foolish children, intent on reaching for a flower over the edge of a cliff. I already knew that kids fell over cliffs and died from all sorts of accidents—my father was a physician—and I wondered why their angels failed them (dramatic tension, noticed early). Also noted was the apparent helplessness of the good, as opposed to the powerful, active energy of evil.

My first foray into the arts was in theatre and, in particular, special effects. Together with one of my brothers, Stephen, I devised an entertainment called 'The Ghost Pants'. Charging sixpence admission, we gathered an audience of our parents, younger siblings and the Taylors from next door. Sitting expectant in a darkened room, they watched as a cupboard door creaked open, and slowly, at first with the odd jerk, a pair of my father's underpants appeared, hovering ghost-like in mid-air before slowly circumnavigating the room and flying out the door. (It's amazing what can be done with black cotton thread and dim lighting.) The performance was a huge success and was talked about (in the family only, alas) for decades.

Why do people want to write? Or, as they often say, 'want to *be* a writer'? Some say it's the desire for 'self-expression'. Perhaps it's because people take notice of writers in a way they don't take notice of lawyers, doctors, dentists and other professional people.

There is a certain éclat in 'being a writer'. For male writers, there is a romance about the profession—the Lord Byron effect—and this can prove very useful for gaining female attention. Women have a soft spot for male writers. (Not sure if the opposite is true regarding women writers and men.) It could be the image—the machismo of Hemingway, the crazy recklessness of Scott Fitzgerald, the shambling, boyish, irresistibility of Dylan Thomas, the bottles of Scotch, the wild, untamed bohemian lifestyle. In contrast, the virginal Emily Dickinson, the Brontës in their modest muslin frocks, Mary Anna Evans and Agatha Christie don't quite summon up the same excitement.

I think a number of factors need to come together to make a writer. A dominating parent and a challenging childhood often go hand in hand; a child whose voice is suppressed, bursting out later in journals and stories. A highly developed imagination is another prerequisite.

Imagination is like language—stop using it and it atrophies or dries up like a well. Use it often and it keeps flowing.

But even that's not enough.

A writer also requires a dogged persistence, a tenacity to keep hanging on until the work is finished. All these factors must be in place, along with the elusive quality called 'talent', which is never enough without the others. The craft of writing can be learned. The talent is a gift.

I started my writing apprenticeship early. I read voraciously and promiscuously: Greek myths, Norse legends, Arthurian romances, Phantom comics, Violet Needham, Noel Streatfeild, my father's collection of forensic jurisprudence books, Enid Blyton, Charles Kingsley, ten volumes of *Newnes' Children's Pictorial Encyclopaedia* and 'Girls' Own' books about hilarious 'rags' in jolly English boarding schools (my first convent boarding school was more like a detention centre—no jolly rags there).

The Greek legends glowed with surprising elements of transformation—sometimes of a very literal sort as deserving mortals morphed into gods and goddesses. I remember questioning my mother about the story of Eros and 'Pish'.

'Who, dear?'

'Pish,' I said.

'Could you spell that please?'

'P-S-Y-C-H-E.'

'Oh *that* Pish,' said my mother.

I can also remember coming across the word 'ocean' for the first time, and being puzzled at its oddness and the way it couldn't be 'sounded out'. It still looks strange to me to this day.

Books and words were a source of constant wonder and getting a new book for Christmas or a birthday filled me with joy. I read under the desk at boarding school, and with a torch beneath the blankets. At Randwick library, I would borrow the permitted three books, and often read an extra one while I was there.

I wrote stories and radio plays before high school, shocking my mother with a particularly violent crime story—now forgotten. I smuggled books into the convent, hiding them in the school library in plain sight under fake Dewey decimals. (Reading material from 'outside' was not permitted. All contraband goods, including sweets and books, had to be declared to the excise nun at the entrance lobby.)

My Irish grandfather entertained us with tales of Billy, who wore boots, and his role as scourge of the kindergarten for little girls run by two ladies, Miss McQuigglepeg and Miss McCorkadale. Billy sabotaged every outing organised for the little girls because he longed to be part of the fun. The Misses McQuigglepeg and McCorkadale might decide to take the little girls to the swimming pool or on a picnic only to find that the plug had been pulled out and the pool emptied; or their picnic ruined by snails in the basket. The culprit was obvious and Billy would be quickly found cowering behind a shed, or hiding up a tree, his dangling boots giving him away. Poor Billy. Always bad, always caught, and always punished.

These simple tales obeyed the classic architecture of storytelling described by Aristotle (and never really improved upon). The three-act structure of drama and tragedy mirrors the movements and transitions of life: the passionate attachments, the jealousies, births and deaths, the obstacles, the reversals that challenge our own lives. Action. Reaction. Resolution. (It is the same structure as a joke . . . and sex.)

I learned about critics very early—and about 'thought crime'. At boarding school I wrote a poem, for *my* eyes only, concerning my confusion and questions about being a girl of fourteen. This was discovered in one of the nuns' early-morning raids (carried out while we were all at mass). We would come back from the chapel to our study room to find desk-lids thrown back, exercise books and textbooks scattered. What were they looking for? Forbidden evils, like hidden chocolate, letters from boys, banned books . . . ? I guess today it might be drugs.

To my immense shame and humiliation, my very private poem was read out to the class with the nun's mocking commentary about some of the less successful similes I employed. I wanted to die.

A diary I'd kept during a retreat was also discovered and with it, my doubts about the existence of God. To be fair to the nuns, this blasphemous and shocking revelation went unpunished, but my dangerous ideas couldn't be allowed to fester. For several weeks, after tea, I was given one-to-one counselling aimed at convincing me of God's existence, based upon the arguments of the great church fathers. Wasted efforts, but I can't blame them for trying. God can't be 'taught', only experienced.

The fiction collection in the convent library ended with the Victorians—George Eliot, Dickens, Thomas Hardy and John Galsworthy's *The Forsyte Saga*, removed some time later. (Soames Forsyte enforcing his conjugal rights was no doubt considered too much for the convent.) I read to escape what was going on around me, finding the world of literature preferable to the reality of boarding-school life.

I didn't attempt to write a novel until I was 22, but it petered out at around 10 000 words and I can't remember anything about it now. In those days, there were no creative writing courses. There was the Fellowship of Australian Writers whose meetings I used to attend on occasion, where people would read out their latest writings and others would comment. I was a young mother by this stage, living in a teacher's residence, attached to a small school run by my husband.

Not long after my failed first attempt at a novel, I opened a biography of Gertrude Stein on a remainder table, and one sentence (the only writing of Stein's I've ever read) jumped out at me:

I decided when I was thirty that I'd write.

Closing the book, I put it back on the table and said to myself, 'So will I.'

The age of 30 was eight years away. I could put off writing a novel while I researched life . . . and research I did.

Anyone who wants to be a writer has to make it their first priority. This means neglecting other important things like family and friends. For years, as I toiled in the now superseded Commonwealth Employment Office, which the local kids called 'the Unemployment Office', from 8.45 a.m. to 5.06 p.m., supporting myself and my daughter Madeleine, I found writing time before and after work.

On my thirtieth birthday, according to that mysterious, inner decision, I'd already started writing a novel. Each morning I'd get up and write for a couple of hours before making my daughter breakfast and getting her ready for school and then going to work. Those cool, dark hours before the dawn, with only the shift workers and the Trappist monks awake, allowed me the space and silence in which to write. I completed a first novel and a large part of a second. Neither was successful, but they were important teaching devices. Most importantly, I learned just to keep going right through to the end.

In 1977 I applied for a New Writers Fellowship, 'peacocking' the best bits out of my second unfinished novel, *A Death in the Family*. To my great surprise, I was awarded a grant of $9000—only a couple of thousand less than my salary in those days. It meant I could take a whole year away from the 'unemployment office' to write full time.

I set about reworking the second novel: a sombre, literary effort about two sisters in Edwardian Australia, living on the Parramatta River. A publisher, now defunct, had asked fellowship winners for a first look and invited me to deliver the manuscript to his office. I did so, expectantly awaiting his phone call, which came some weeks later. He sat me down, poured me a double scotch, and read me the reader's report. It was very succinct and I still remember every word of it:

> *Mrs Lord has looked into the wood shed, seen something nasty, thought it was life, and written about it.*

I was deeply dejected. I had three weeks left before the Fellowship ran out, at which time I would have to report for duty at Penrith CES office. In a blazing pique, I sat down and wrote *Fortress*. I have never worked so quickly nor been more focused, sustained by a driving *I'll show them* fury.

That small novel was an international bestseller, going into dozens of languages and editions. It came out in 1980 when the only other 'crime novel' in Australia was Peter Corris's *The Empty Beach*. Coincidentally, both books were made into films, Peter's starring Bryan Brown, while Rachel Ward took the lead role in *Fortress*. She played the young schoolteacher at a small rural school whose students are kidnapped by gun-wielding thugs. Apart from the 1996 telemovie of *Whipping Boy*, it was almost 30 years before I had that kind of international success again when my young adult series, *Conspiracy 365*, was transformed into a high-quality TV series.

Lest people think that a bestselling book can be written in three weeks, I need to add that I'd been thinking about this story for about eight years, ever since nine nurses were murdered in Chicago after tying each other up, as the knife-wielding perpetrator commanded. At around the same time, a young schoolteacher at Faraday, Victoria, was kidnapped along with about a dozen children. She refused to obey orders from the kidnappers and managed to escape with her charges. The tension between these two stories—of young nurses who died when they obeyed their kidnapper, and a young woman who survived when she disobeyed—created a question in me that I partly answered by writing *Fortress*.

The success of that first novel catapulted me from the obscurity of a rented house in Castle Hill into the ranks of Sydney's literati. I remember crazy nights at Kinselas with Jean Bedford and other fine people, picking a wine from the wine list without looking. This 'lottery' could result in a local drop worth several dollars a bottle or an imported wine worth 80 or 90.

I recall one night where one of the Davids (I can't remember if it was Ireland or Foster) was crawling under the table biting people's ankles. These were the days when I owned a full-body leopard-print leotard (naturally with a tail), which I occasionally lashed around in.

My first publisher and his wife, thoroughly decent people whom I shall call the 'X's, gave generous and interesting dinner parties. This worldly and kindly couple evoked in me a deep self-consciousness. For some reason, I always felt that I would do something terribly inappropriate in their company, like fart loudly or swear or spill red wine on their pale apple green carpet. (I never wore the leopard print leotard in their company.) After one such anxiety-ridden dinner (during which I and the other three guests drank quite a lot), the four of us staggered out into the night looking for a taxi or two. I don't know if he'll remember this, but Barry Oakley, a perfect velvet-jacketed gentlemen, threw back his head and roared out into the night on a rising crescendo: 'Root! Suck! Fuck!

Cunt! Chunder!!!!' Startled, we asked him what had brought on this surprising chorus. 'Oh,' he explained. 'I always feel like that after dining with the Xs.' I can't express how grateful and delighted I felt hearing this. I wasn't the only one. Thank you, Barry.

Pretty soon I discovered that once you've written one book, publishers always want another one. The second book is always hard, especially when the first has been an international bestseller. My second novel was quietly received—only the French bought it—then came a third and so on.

After six stand-alone novels, I found myself revisiting the two sisters, Kit Westlake and Gemma Lincoln, who first appeared in *Feeding the Demons*. I liked these two characters so much that I wanted to know what had happened to them in the interim. That's how the Gemma Lincoln private investigator series developed. I didn't have a clue what a PI did, apart from what I'd read in the newspapers, but a close association with a senior detective in the NSW Police physical evidence section (the old scientific squad) proved invaluable. From him I gained access to photographs and crime scene videos that I probably shouldn't have seen. In addition, I learned about forensics such as blood spray patterns.

'Okay, Gabes,' he'd say if we came across some interesting paint stains on a pavement. He pointed out the elliptical and exclamation mark-like trajectories. 'Now what does this tell us about the direction of the blows?'

One particular crime scene photograph showed a pair of strange two-dimensional 'figures' of a man and a woman laid out on the floor of a bedroom. They were made out of clothes—a pair of jeans, with a shirt on top representing the man, lying beside a dress with stockings emerging from under the skirt creating the female figure. From the open fly of the 'man's' jeans, a tie snaked its way under the dress.

A second photograph showed the dress being lifted away to reveal a bra and panties arranged on the carpet like an empty bikini, with talcum powder on the floor where the 'armpits' might have been. Police found a damp semen stain on the dress and nearby an empty cereal box that had been stabbed multiple times with a knife.

This offender would creep into women's houses while they were asleep and set up his little piece of masturbatory theatre, using clothes from the women's cupboards. Looking at the crime scene photographs, I had the clear impression that this guy hadn't quite got his act together. He was still fantasising about what he wanted to do, moving closer with each day to having a living, breathing woman beneath his knife. Imagine waking up one morning and discovering this on your floor, I asked myself. Thus began *Feeding the Demons*.

Even with murder, research is everything. For example, if you're planning to murder your wife and make it look like a rapist carried out the crime, you had better study dozens of genuine rape and murder crime scenes. Get it right or an experienced investigator can tell almost at a glance whether it's the real deal or a set-up. They use the same skills and techniques as the currency experts in the old counterfeit money squad. Instead of looking at fake banknotes, they would spend months studying the genuine article until they knew every detail. They spotted the fakes by recognising what was real—rather than the other way around.

For my own research, I did 'work experience' in a small private security firm, run by a well-known ex-detective. I went out on surveillance and got a first-hand understanding of how extremely boring it is. I used subterfuge to assess someone's identity. I listened to tales of various stings carried out on cheating men by the ex-detective's beautiful, highly educated daughter. 'I do a great bimbo,' she told me. Her department was a service called 'Mancheck', from which derives Gemma Lincoln's fictional service 'Mandate', checking the bona fides of new romantic interests for busy career women.

Other research saw me spend time with DNA analysts, homicide detectives, child abuse experts and weapons inspectors. I have learned how to make anthrax (although not how to weaponise it). I have taken flying lessons, spent a day with the dog squad and heard from customs officers about 'stuffers' and 'swallowers' and the connection between criminals and parrots.

I've spent time at the morgue being briefed by pathologists and other experts, or sitting in the bone room where the skeletal remains of long dead and anonymous victims await identification. I was so moved by these poignant fragments of a human being's life—a handful of bones and a withered sandal—that I almost called the novel *The Bone Room*.

For a year I studied anatomy at Sydney University, fascinated by the marvellous human body and its systems of pipes, pumps, pouches, pulleys, levers and organs. I forked out money and spent an intensive week holed up in a Canberra hotel, learning SCAN—Scientific Content Analysis, an Israeli system for detecting deception in verbal and written statements using only close textual examination, noticing the subtle red flags in the language that betray the writer or speaker.

'Do not use this on your friends or relatives,' warned the trainer, 'or soon you will not have any friends or relatives.'

This research was important, but before any of this knowledge can be put to use, I need the seed of an idea that my imagination can work on. As I've mentioned, this might come from a crime scene photograph, or a piece of music, or just a question such as, 'How far might a woman go to stay young and beautiful?'

This is the question that I sought to answer in *Death by Beauty*, my latest Gemma Lincoln novel. The story grew in stages, from the notes to the research, to the plotting, through to the end. Bringing such a large work to completion takes a lot of brain energy. In particular to create a climax that Hitchcock described as having a 'surprising inevitability'. Readers should gasp, 'Oh no!' followed immediately by 'Of course!'

Some folk dismiss this as 'formulaic' and so it is in a sense—in the same way that knitting a jumper is formulaic—it follows certain principles. There have to be two knitted sleeves, a back and a front, an opening for the neck. By all means, throw the rules away and write experimentally, but just keep that jumper in mind—five sleeves, no neck opening and an uneven hem might be brilliantly different and original, but will anyone ever want to wear it?

The writing is really only about ten per cent of it. For me, the real work, the hard part, is in the structure and building of the story. This can be done as one writes, of course, or by working from the pre-built plan, like a map. A novel creates a world in my mind that didn't exist before and it only starts happening with time and patience. This is why burgeoning writers are often advised: just write something, anything, but do it every day. Show up and sit there, start anywhere. Just start.

I write because I have something to say and I really enjoy saying it. Maybe that's what happens to someone who was not permitted to speak in her own defence in childhood. I derive great pleasure and satisfaction from taking a whole lot of chaotic ideas and strands and characters and organising them into some kind of order.

Storytelling is the other, oldest profession. Scheherazade literally kept her head with constant cliff-hanging stories for a thousand and one nights, thereby winning the dubious prize of becoming the sultan's umpteenth wife.

Recently I watched author Garth Nix keep a large adult audience transfixed as he narrated his dangerous brush with a group of brigands on the Afghan–Pakistan border during a somewhat foolhardy trip to the area. Rolling up his sleeves, he showed the faded bruising occasioned by his narrow escape from these ruffians. It was storytelling at its most compelling. As the spellbound audience gaped in horrified wonder at the bruises, Garth revealed that he'd made up the whole thing, and the bruises had been rubbed onto his forearms moments before his presentation using biro. We humans are hardwired to respond to hearing about other people's experiences—even fictionalised experience.

Ideas are ten a penny. The execution of an idea into a novel is quite another matter. At festivals and other venues where writers come out of their natural isolation and mingle with readers, I'm sometimes approached by someone who says, 'I've got this fantastic idea for a book! Why don't you write it?'

In fact, quite recently, I heard of a writer approached by someone with 'a great idea' and the suggestion that she write the book based on the great idea, and they'd go 50/50 in the proceeds! Great ideas abound. Pick up a newspaper, listen to conversations on the bus, daydream, read, watch movies, scrutinise your own family—the air teems with information. Just as the Sigintel operatives pull information out of the electronic signals crowding the air waves and weave it together to make an intelligible, integrated whole, a writer's job is to pull the story out of all the noise and movement emanating from the world channel, and wrangle it together with the internal world to make a comprehensive story.

Do all of these things and finally, inevitably, you may find yourself looking at a completed first draft. Once that's happened, I sigh with relief. It doesn't matter if it's a complete mess—there's something now in existence that can be worked on, worried at, pulled around, rewritten, rejigged, scrapped, replaced, until finally there's a draft ready to go to the editors.

That's when the real fun begins. It's not unusual to get four or five closely typed pages stapled together, listing perhaps 40 or 50 points that I have to address. This just has to be endured, slowly worked through, because usually the editors are right. They've spotted the weaknesses, the place where the plot creaks, or that the colour of the dress changes mysteriously.

Once I was staying with Jean Bedford and Peter Corris at one of their serial coastal houses and Peter was working through an edited manuscript in a small room at the back of the house. From time to time, cries of 'Fuck you, Murray!' (I can't remember the real name and it's probably just as well) rang through the house.

'Pete's rewriting,' Jean explained. I nodded. I knew the feeling.

MY RULES

1. **Make writing your first priority.**

   It comes before everything else.

2. **Don't wait until 'I have enough time'.**

   Make time! Do it now! Anyone can get up at 4 a.m. and do a couple of hours.

3. **Be kind to yourself.**

   Don't expect that first draft will be anything but a horrible mess. That's the job of a first draft—to see what a muddle you're in. But the elements of your story might be somewhere in the mess.

4. **Be prepared to do a lot of rewriting.**

5. **Do sufficient research so that you feel confident when writing about something.**

   You don't have to be an expert, just observant. When I visited DAL, the Division of Analytic Laboratories, I noticed how the rape victims' panties had been pinned out like big butterflies on what looked like breadboards, prior to samples being cut. That sort of telling detail can only enrich your story.

6. Make a commitment that you will finish this thing, even if you're not happy with it.

You're not supposed to be happy with it. That's called writing. It needs to be worked on until you are happy with it.

7. Don't buy 'writer's block'.

This just means you haven't worked out your story properly yet. Keep asking yourself, 'And then what happens?' If you find yourself answering, 'I don't know' say sternly, 'You're not leaving this desk until you find out!'

8. You are free to write anything and in any way you choose.

But if you want people to read your books, you need to write something that people want to read. Save the deconstructed, post-modernist version of Ulysses *from the points of view of ten unreliable narrators for impressing the impressionable.*

9. You can only write what you know.

So live life, as fully and richly as you can.

10. Keep in mind there is a mystery at the heart of things (which includes writing).

Let the unconscious creative forces work for you. Sometimes, the answer to a plot problem will just jump into your mind from where it's been brooding beyond your conscious ken. Be grateful when that happens.

FIVE MUST-READS

1. The Greek myths

2. The Poetics of Aristotle *by Aristotle*

3. Dip into translations of early English elegies *and also* **Beowulf** *(for an excellent example of failed dramatic structure)*

4. Shakespeare

5. Lots of good poets from every epoch

*Gabrielle Lord is often referred to as Australia's first
lady of crime, having written fifteen crime novels and
a twelve-volume thriller series for young adults. Her
first novel,* Fortress, *was a huge international success
and was made into a feature film starring Rachel Ward.
She is a past winner of the Ned Kelly Award for
Crime Fiction and the recipient of a Lifetime Achievement
Award from the Australian Crime Writers Association.
She is currently writing Books 16 and 17 of the
Conspiracy 365 series for Young Adults.*
www.gabriellelord.com

THE FACTS, MA'AM, NOTHING BUT THE FACTS

By Lindsay Simpson

Walking the inner-city streets of Toronto, I struggle to explain to a fellow academic when I first became fascinated by crime. We are passing The Hair of the Dog, a neighbourhood pub in this gay district of Toronto, a suitably sleazy backdrop. It is a story I have told before. Tonight, though, I struggle with the memory of it. It doesn't slip off the tongue like it used to. Or maybe, I have forgotten key parts of the story.

There was a book—I remember—about the Christie murders. The sheer horror of trying to imagine how the victims had suffered, what final words they may have uttered. I remember my father regaling me with its contents. We were still living in Ayrshire, Scotland, which means I was less than ten years old. That's when we left the place of my birth.

Then there was another book: a picture book read under the sheets by torchlight at boarding school in Swaziland, southern Africa. A book with black-and-white photographs which graphically depicted how people met their grisly ends. Where that book came from is anyone's guess. I only remember that it mattered to me, even then, that these stories were 'true'; that these black-and-white photographs were graphic renditions of what had actually happened.

From an early age, I felt the appeal of the gritty details, 'the facts ma'am and nothing but the facts'. Crime fiction never captured my imagination in this way. It was always the poor cousin. Why would you invent a story when truth, so the hackneyed phrase tells us, is stranger than fiction?

In our family, the Scottish-accented 'tut-tut' inevitably preceded an account around the dinner table of the latest murder story from the newspaper headlines. The details were enough to stop an evening meal. My grandmother, who turned 100 this year, has always been a keen observer of crime. She has a predilection for the magazine *That's Life*, with all its ramped-up sensationalism. Ever the storyteller, I learned from her, while sipping her Scotch broth with 'tatties' at her kitchen table, how to spin a yarn—and dark yarns at that.

The crossroads in my life, which was to be a harbinger of things to come, was a lunch—around 1985—in Kings Cross, Sydney, with the then *Sydney Morning Herald* editor, Eric Beecher. He was a very disarming man who dressed like an accountant—white shirt, inoffensive tie and prosaic navy or beige pants (even his glasses were respectable)—yet it was rare to have a relaxing conversation with Beecher. His mouth, with an occasional grimace, would fire staccato questions like missiles.

I soon discovered the best time of the day to do business with him, which meant 'selling' your story and bypassing news conference, was at 5 p.m. when the editor's secretary had gone and before the mad evening rush of final deadlines. Beecher had a habit, back then, of dismissing you by glancing meaningfully at the clock above the door in his office. Just prior to that fateful lunch, he had sent me to live on the streets of Kings Cross for three weeks. Robert Thomson, who went on to become editor of the *Wall Street Journal*, was sent on a similar expedition—but his brief was to live in Redfern to sketch out his version of life on those streets.

Back in those heady days, money was still being spent on investigative journalism, financed by the paper's 'rivers of gold' (classified advertising). This even extended to *Herald* drivers delivering extra cash to the Astoria Hotel on the main drag where the photographer and I were holed up entertaining 'trannies' and prostitutes with a fridge full of alcohol.

There was a slush fund, too, for defamation cases to help investigative journalists go 'close to the edge'. Although never discussed publicly, this meant that particular journalists were backed by the newspaper to run close to (or over) the line to 'get the big guys, those outside of the arm of the law'.

During my three weeks at the Cross, I would lie in bed reading George Orwell's published letters, intoxicated with the romance of becoming a writer, albeit not exactly living the life of the tramp. My only brief was to write about what I saw, collecting ordinary people's stories in an era before reality television, user-generated content and YouTube. Each day challenged my resourcefulness to capture the pulse of the ever-changing strip that was Kings Cross.

The photographer and I would work all night, visiting the change rooms of strip joints to photograph the strippers (often males impersonating females) getting dressed again after the gig (the photographer's idea). Or we would visit the boys-own brothels, where the male prostitutes disparagingly labelled their female counterparts as 'mattresses' because all they had to do was lie back and think of the Queen.

At Salon Kitty, the girls were university students who never slept with their clients. Orgasms were generally not permitted unless they were part of the fantasy storyboard. The clientele were judges and lawyers whose dreams were delivered literally in the form of earth arriving in trucks to bury them alive or real scalpels being used to feign surgical procedures. There was even an adult-sized paddling pool where men in over-sized bonnets would happily splash while receiving slaps from the girls who only had to expose nipples to receive a pay-packet quadruple what the girls across the road received (girls who were mostly heroin addicts working for a fix).

As a journalist, the proviso of entry into this successful establishment was never to go near the front door when the clients arrived, lest they be recognised. Once I did encounter a plump man dressed in a tutu who was paying $150 per hour to get dressed by the girls to wander the streets of the Cross. He had still not 'come out' to his wife.

'Whatever you do, you must not laugh,' I was warned by one of the madams.

Returning with photographs to thank the girls, I was sent up to the Titanic room to check out the latest 'fantasy' creation. A masked woman, dressed in leathers and wielding a whip, flung open the door commanding the photographer and me to come inside. A naked man was crouched, bound and gagged in a corner of the room. 'Lovely colour scheme,' I said, avoiding the face attached to the buttocks in case I recognised it. (Why would you bother making all of this up?)

I came up with a price list for the newspaper series based on the sexual activities on offer—a veritable smorgasbord of the bizarre and mundane all priced by the hour. Having read the three-part series, ever-tetchy Beecher declared airily that the stories were far too focused on sex.

'Well, you did send me to the red-light district,' I said, pointing out that I had, at least, unearthed a 'garbologist', the first of the recyclers who despised his neighbour because he hoarded and could no longer get through his front door.

Beecher wanted me to frame the stories on a broader canvas. Grudgingly, I returned to William Street finding two survivors from the Holocaust, long-term dwellers in the Cross, who lived outside of the suburb's main economic paradigm. They certainly had a story to tell.

I had guessed that the lunch that day was to reward my ingenuity. Beecher chose his haunt, Bayswater Brasserie, and waited until his penne arrabbiata had arrived before clearing his throat.

'I can imagine you as an Edna O'Brien,' he said. 'She's the reporter from the *Miami Herald* who drives around with a gun in her boot.'

I had never heard of Edna O'Brien and certainly didn't have a gun in my boot. I didn't have a gun licence. What was he talking about?

'I thought you might want to become the *Herald*'s first female Chief-Police reporter,' he said.

My first reaction was one of shock. Up until that moment I'd been daydreaming about my newfound roots in literary journalism, but those dreams came crashing to earth. Pushing pasta around my plate, I asked myself where I'd find time to dwell on the well-crafted sentence or the extended metaphor. After all, Flaubert had taken five years to write one sentence and Orwell immersed himself in the worlds he wrote about. News reporting left little time for that.

'Mmm . . .'

But ever-prescient Beecher foresaw more than the next day's fish-and-chip wrapping. With that offer, he became responsible for my future literary efforts being directed towards the true crime genre. My first appearance at the daily news conference was viewed with great suspicion, not least because, in the mid-1980s, there were few women around the table and also because crime rarely made page one of the *Herald*. That was the domain of the tabloids.

My contacts in the criminal milieu, which established my credentials, began in the courts. My first case as a young cadet was a charge of road rage. The prosecutor held up a bloodied hand-knitted jumper belonging to the victim who had been dragged from his Telecom van and bashed by a fellow motorist after changing lanes one too many times. I was transfixed. I loved the theatrics of it all. The ceremony. The grandstanding. The lies.

When the evidence dried up, or the jury had retired to deliberate on their verdict, I would jump into a taxi and visit the dark-bricked Coroner's Court to check on an inquest; or dash up to the sandstone-pillared Supreme Court at 'Darlo' for a chilling outline of the prosecution case in the latest murder trial.

One of my early cases involved filing my copy from a phone box outside the Darlo courts for the *Sun* reporter. The story was 'the Busby Ripper', who had killed several women while masquerading as a pest exterminator. My early favours for that reporter were later reciprocated when he was hired as a TV reporter and would feed me morsels: stories without visuals.

There were some poignant cases: a woman in her thirties who sweetly smiled at the jurors when they arrived each morning, thanking them for coming. She had been charged with grievous bodily harm after opening up her five-year-old daughter's pyjama top and stabbing her with a pair of scissors. The nine-year-old sibling had called the ambulance. Her daughter's letter forgiving her mother was read to the court before the judge abruptly dismissed the case citing sanity as a major issue.

In those early court-reporting days, one story stood out from the run-of-the-mill celebrity-driving offences, judges on trial and brutal murders. It was the tale of two private schoolboys who decided one day to rob a bank. They made a pact. If they were caught, they would use their own guns to kill themselves. But it was the entries in their diaries that caught my imagination—the quotes from Kafka and Sartre, their 'noble aspirations' to end it all—the kind of existential angst I discovered reading Dostoevsky as an undergraduate. They *were* caught. A traffic police constable happened to be riding past on his motorbike. One of the boys pointed the gun under his bike helmet and blew his brains out. Standing on top of the tellers' bench, the other tried, but he only partially managed it. He ended up in a wheelchair. A few months later, he booked himself into the Camperdown Travelodge in inner Sydney and killed himself.

I tracked down the doctor who had treated him as a paraplegic (the doctor happened to be the father of one of my colleagues). I was struck by the honesty and the openness of the doctor and captivated by a tragedy that seemed almost Shakespearean. The yawning life of the story outside of the courtroom needed telling.

My daily news grind, however, distracted me from my main aim to become a writer. In the meantime, I was striking up friendships with a rich array of characters. In the subterranean worlds I inhabited, I convinced two rape victims of the same serial rapist to meet for a story. I also had my white sunglasses jumped upon by a homicide detective, who promptly shoved a twenty-dollar note in my bag to apologise for his unprovoked rage. I met a hit man in the pouring rain outside the National Crime Authority (he refused to meet in a café or bar lest I tip off his whereabouts to person or persons unknown). Named 'Black George', he always sat with his back to the wall and bragged that he had only ever served time for one murder.

Another case that ricocheted into my world will be forever known as the 'Milperra Father's Day Massacre'. Seven people were shot dead at a swap meet on Father's Day during a shootout between two rival bikie gangs— the Bandidos and the Comancheros. It was the first mass shooting, outside of colonial times, to happen in Australia. Covering the first day of the court case, wedged next to the Bandidos whose dock extended to the boundary of the media section, I was completely hooked by the personalities and details that emerged. So was another young woman, Sandra Harvey, who was filing hourly updates for AAP. Over coffee breaks, we confided to each other that we'd always wanted to be writers. So, our friendship, and commitment to the story, was born. This unexpected pairing was to last 24 years, until Sandra's death in January 2008. Together we produced three crime books, beginning with *Brothers in Arms*.

Turning our backs on the pursuit of the page-one lead, we committed ourselves to a much nobler pursuit: the immortal book. In the background, while performing the daily grind and meeting deadlines, we began to fossick for contacts, passing Minties to the Bandidos inside the courtroom. Soon afterwards, Sandra received the first letter from Commonwealth gold boxing medallist

'Knuckles' McElwaine, one of the gang members. This was the beginning of our long association with these 'real' characters. His brother, Gloves, offered to take me on the back of his Harley once he got out of prison and we could 'putt putt' down the highway.

After the daily court proceedings finished, we would be taken back to the office in a white Mercedes driven by a man with a burnt face. In the front seat was the Bandidos' lawyer, Chris Murphy, the man who had VERBAL as his number plate. We would eat pistachios and drink gin and tonics, soaking up a different world. This time, the story did not end when the court case finished. I had entered the world of books and my dreams of being a literary scribe had been hijacked by something that seemed bigger than fate. I had been placed smack-bang in the middle of life itself.

Truman Capote's *In Cold Blood* provided the exact template Sandra and I sought—the literary rendition of a crime and the immersion of the writer in the story. We both always fancied the turn of phrase and the lure of the romance of the writer. It is fashionable today for academics to denigrate Capote. At the academic conference in Toronto, there was a competition on whether Hersey or Capote was worse for making things up.

Capote's approach of getting close and personal with the criminals, however, instead of portraying them as faceless figures or stereotypes, shouldn't be challenged and it led us to appropriating the quote from Jean Genet's

The Thief's Journal, which we placed at the beginning of *Brothers in Arms*:

> *Though they may not always be handsome, men doomed to evil possess the manly virtues. Of their own volition, or owing to an accident which has been chosen for them, they plunge lucidly and without complaint into a reproachful, ignominious element, like that into which love, if it is profound, hurls human beings.*

Genet's comment echoed Dostoevsky's fatalistic account of Raskolnikov in *Crime and Punishment* that had so fascinated me in my undergraduate days. This quote captures the essence of why I write true crime. It is the serendipitous nature of the act. How much depends on the events leading up to a fatal encounter: how one person looking out of his window and noticing a rival gang ride by leads to seven people being shot dead in a hotel carpark. How a man who had never killed a rabbit before is able to be convinced to shoot an innocent woman; and how a serial killer's lust for killing is set off by the colour his victim has chosen to dye her hair.

True crime always provides the unexpected: the twists and turns of the plot, the depth of the characters, the complexity of the relationships and the vagaries of human nature. Shaking the hand of a serial killer in jail, before beginning the first of fourteen interviews over a period of six months, I knew that nobody else was concerned with 'why' because this man had been convicted. I loved the thrill of the chase, the second-guessing of the plot and immersion into other worlds.

I have attended a Gangster & Moll party run by the Black Uhlans, and learned how to dive in a gloomy quarry in Birmingham, Alabama, with the same dive instructor who taught Tina Watson—the young bride who died on her scuba-diving honeymoon. Her husband, Gabe, was later charged with her murder and eventually acquitted after legal proceedings that crossed two continents.

Retelling these stories has often challenged my pre-conceptions. I remember how Sandra and I longed to live the uncomplicated lives of bikie old ladies: cooking for your man and minding the kids. It seemed like a panacea for our generation of superwomen, who thought that 'doing everything' meant equality of the sexes.

Curiosity is an essential characteristic for the true crime writer. Wanting to understand why. Writing 'true crime' provides scenarios that the imagination could never conjure. Real people have complexities and contradictions that defy their fictional counterparts.

As I begin my sixth book in the genre, I am already immersed in the puzzle. I'm driving through a forest to where a young boy's remains have been found almost ten years after he went missing. I have visited the bus stop where he was last seen, recording the details I know I will use in the writing of the story. Each day I am piecing together events and collecting those small details that I know will be significant as I reconstruct the past and allow the story to slowly materialise.

Books can explore crimes in a way that newspapers can never hope to achieve. Not just contemporary tales, but historical mysteries. There is one story I have promised my 100-year-old grandmother that I *will* tell. It is the tale of her own father (my great-grandfather), who was a soldier and gravedigger in the First World War. Family folklore has it that he was murdered in France in November 1920.

Playing detective, I have pieced together some of the story. After volunteering as 'a territorial' and surviving through four years as a stretcher-bearer, Sergeant Robert Grant stayed on as a gravedigger with the Canadian clearing-houses. He was only 35 when he died under mysterious circumstances just before he was due to go home to Inverness to celebrate Christmas.

My grandmother was eight years old and remembers the telegram boy cycling up the road towards their house—an omen in wartimes. The First World War had ended, yet here was the telegram boy again—a phantom from the past heralding death.

I have made a career of discovering others' secrets, but would I be able to uncover our own? I am the first and only member of my family to visit my great-grandfather's grave in Duisans, near Arras in France, close to the Belgian border. Sergeant Robert Grant was one of the last soldiers to be buried in one of the mass Commonwealth graveyards where the fallen lie together in perpetuity. Would he have wanted such a public outing?

Plagued with doubt, I ponder this in the five-kilometre cycle ride to the graveyard where red poppies still line the roadside. I pick one to place on his grave. With more than 3000 headstones to search, my eyes are like a mine-sweeper going from left to right. His grave is one of the last to be erected in the far north of the graveyard under a spreading oak. The engraved words on his headstone are like a personal missive. They hit me in the heart and tears spring from nowhere:

> *From memory's page, Time Cannot Blot, Three Little Words Forget Him Not.*

After decades of writing true crime, I am on the trail of a very personal story, perhaps the most challenging project I have ever undertaken.

In the newspaper office of Arras, I begin reading the archives of *La Voix du Nord*, facing a seemingly impossible task of finding a newspaper story on a murdered soldier in a war where 16 million lives were lost. But it is the thrill of the chase that drives me—the chance to discover something that has been hidden for nearly a century. As I walk the streets of Arras, visiting the bunkers and the hollowed-out grass knolls created by shells fired so long ago, I know that this story contains the essential elements that motivate me to write crime. To leave no stone unturned, a tenacity honed by years as an investigative journalist; to come as close as I possibly can to reconstruct the past and to get the truth onto the page.

MY RULES

1. *Make your life fit around your writing time, not your writing time around your life.*

2. *Don't complain if you haven't done the above.*

3. *Trust your instinct for a story.*

4. *Try your book ideas out at parties,*
   but not enough that people will get bored (or worse still, that you will).

5. *If writing true crime, try walking into a story with no preconceptions.*

6. *Visit the place you are writing about.*
   (That's jails, dive quarries, quaint Croatian villages.)

7. *Listen for dialogue and watch for mannerisms—*
   use your phone to record impressions.

8. *Writing true crime:*
   find as many documents as you can to recreate scenes, dialogue, characters, and swear allegiance to the truth and nothing but the truth as far as you are able to represent.

9. **Be prepared to meet and engage with lots of interesting characters,**
   and rise to the challenge of capturing them in the written word.

10. **Be prepared to invest a lot of time in the digital world of ebooks and social networking,**
    to connect to a world full of potential readers.

FIVE MUST-READS

1. **Possession** *by A.S. Byatt*
2. **The Alexandria Quartet** *by Lawrence Durrell*
3. **The God of Small Things** *by Arundhati Roy*
4. **The English Patient** *by Michael Ondaatje*
5. **Crime and Punishment** *by Fyodor Dostoevsky*

Lindsay Simpson is an Australian journalist and academic and a writer specialising in true crime. She worked as an investigative journalist for the Sydney Morning Herald *for twelve years and has written or co-authored seven books, including* Honeymoon Dive *and* Brothers in Arms, *recently screened as a mini-series:* Bike Wars: Brothers in Arms. *She is now working as a full-time writer. Her latest book is about the abduction and murder of Daniel Morcombe on Queensland's Sunshine Coast.*

THE NED KELLY AWARDS

by Peter Lawrance

I recall sitting in my car in peak-hour traffic one morning in the mid-1990s, half-listening to the ABC radio program AM, becoming anxious about the time. I was due at work in five minutes and the traffic lights up ahead were flashing amber. Vehicles had banked up and like every other driver I was willing for a break to just 'happen' and get us through.

Peter Thompson, the AM program anchor, announced his last story of the program—a report about a new literary award being launched in Australia. One of the people behind its formation, Stuart Coupe, was on the line. Suddenly, my focus shifted from the torpid traffic to the unfolding interview. This was unusual, exciting news—an award to recognise the best of Australian crime writing: the birth of the Ned Kelly Awards.

By 1996, the year the inaugural awards were presented in Sydney, the state of Australian crime writing was pretty impressive. There had been a 'renaissance' in the genre, thanks in large part to the groundbreaking work of Peter Corris and Gabrielle Lord. Corris, whose first Cliff Hardy novel, *The Dying Trade*, appeared in 1980, introduced readers to the ubiquitous Cliff Hardy, a character who would become synonymous with Australian crime fiction. Three Hardys later came the advent of what might be termed the first defining point in contemporary Australian crime fiction.

The Empty Beach was remarkable on a number of fronts, including storytelling, character and the exploration of social issues and lifestyles. Cliff Hardy spoke in an authentic, sometimes weary Australian voice, and Corris explored aspects of class structure that highlighted the divide between the wealthy and 'the battlers', to use contemporary political parlance.

Corris did more than capture a mood. While writing this essay I chanced upon a newspaper story about a man who caused outrage after he photographed meals in a retirement home. In *The Empty Beach* a scene depicts residents in a similar place of care, being fed from cans of pet food.

The novel went on to be developed and turned into a feature film, again a sign of the momentum the book had generated. In the same time frame, Gabrielle Lord had made an indelible mark with her early crime writing. Her novel *Fortress* (1980) was immensely successful, as were her subsequent thrillers, including *Tooth and Claw* (1983) and *Jumbo* (1986).

If these writers were kicking open the door, other writers came flooding in—new voices and talent—indicating what could be done when Australian authors turned to crime. Not only had the writers arrived, but a willing audience was uncovered and they were hungry for more. That surge was rapidly becoming a wave.

The second defining point in this brief history of Australian crime writing was the appearance of Marele Day in the latter part of the 1980s. Her private detective series featuring Claudia Valentine took the unprecedented step in Australia of placing a woman in a role that had traditionally been a male preserve—the private detective. Day went on to write four Valentine novels. Others were emboldened and followed suit. Gabrielle Lord created Gemma Lincoln, Leigh Redhead gave us stripper-turned-PI Simone Kirsch, and Tara Moss produced the Mak Vanderwall series.

Whether the idea of creating an award for crime writing can be attributed to any one individual is a moot point. The decision was made at a now famous meeting in a Malaysian restaurant at the top end of George Street in Sydney. Present at the gathering were Peter Milne from Abbey's bookshop, academic Noel King, crime novelist John Dale and Stuart Coupe, journalist and co-founder/co-editor of *Mean Streets* crime magazine.

A year or so later—following the first Ned Kelly Awards presentation—I 'happened' upon a similar meeting at possibly the same venue. At the table on this occasion was Marele Day.

The second Ned Kelly Awards took place in Melbourne. This would be my first involvement on the organisational side. My part was to set up the venue at the fabled Continental Café in Prahran, a venue for music performance that had become something of an institution in Melbourne. The Ned Kelly's coming to Melbourne was going to be a big event. That part was easy to sell. The Continental people kindly 'lent' us the actual venue, upstairs. Staff were put on to tend the bar and direct guests to seats. A small stage was set up for the presentations. A contingent of interstate visitors, headed by Denise Yates and her daughters, was travelling down by train especially to collect the Lifetime Achievement award on behalf of the late Alan Yates, known around the world as Carter Brown.

It was a rainy Sunday afternoon as I stood with Stuart Coupe and greeted the arrivals: the Yates family, Peter Temple and Shane Maloney. So we had the winners, we had a few family members, a couple of friends and the bar staff standing around looking expectant. For some reason the 'others' didn't show. Maybe it was the weather?

The following year the Ned Kelly Awards were 'rested'—a euphemism perhaps for no-one being able to summon the energy to take on the task of organisation.

In 1999, at the behest of Peter Doyle and John Dale in Sydney, we tried again. They were held in the bookshop of a large department store in the heart of Sydney. On this occasion the event was a raging success. An audience arrived, wine was served, other people from the store drifted in to see what was happening. Members of the public mingled with a 'who's who' of local crime writers, as well as Ian Rankin, who was visiting Australia to promote his latest Rebus novel.

A month later I had a call from Peter Doyle, posing the idea of the awards returning to Melbourne for the following year. In due course 'paperwork' arrived and the task had to begin.

At around that time in Melbourne, a new magazine devoted to crime writing had been launched. *Crime Factory* was conceived and produced by David Honeybone, who had expressed interest in getting involved in the Neds (an involvement he took to with gusto, maintaining the CWAA and directing the awards over the next couple of years).

In August 2000 we produced our first award ceremony. We wrote to the Melbourne Writers Festival hoping to be part of their program and were granted umbrella status. In the meantime, we found a 'home' at Henry Maas's nightclub, The Night Cat, in Fitzroy. Suddenly things were taking off.

This event established a 'blue-print' for the awards, adding an entertainment element in the hope of drawing a bigger audience. The Ned Kelly Debate was born. Two teams of four, made up of writers, journalists and members of the legal fraternity, debated the premise 'That crime fiction is more interesting than fact'. The event was emceed by Dave Graney and ABC radio had a recording team to capture this 'special' event. An edited version was broadcast several weeks later (by which time some of the wilder stories and bluer idioms had been excised). Language proved no barrier to the crowd, who became happier still when someone plonked a couple of hundred dollars on the bar.

It was during that first debate that panellist Shane Maloney contended that crime fiction 'has become the one place in contemporary writing where you can still be sure of finding moralism at work, if not morality'. He also argued, 'Moralism, like communism, and indeed alcoholism, is an inexact science . . . the crime writer is now in many ways an historian whose research reaches those parts that other histories don't.'

If Maloney's words reflected on aspects of the crime writer's craft, the ongoing history of the awards has revealed the depth of talent at work in Australia. Where the voices of Corris, Lord and Day guided readers through the 1980s and 1990s, a plethora of new voices have emerged in the years since, and Australian crime writing has become a fixture in libraries, bookshops and at literary festivals. In addition to this, Australian crime titles have made it onto school and university curriculums and been published around the world.

The popularity of the genre is reflected in the Ned Kelly Awards. The number of entries has increased each year in all three categories: best first fiction, best fiction and best nonfiction. New names and new voices have emerged, some coming through the major publishing houses, others from smaller, independent companies, along with a handful of self-published works. Throughout this time there have been a number of consistent entrants—authors who have gone on to define the genre in Australia and set exacting standards in the process.

Peter Temple became a serial winner of the Ned Kelly Awards, standing at the podium on one occasion as he clutched the heavy metal statue and quipping about its potential worth as a possible projectile. And of course Temple would go on to win other prestigious prizes, including the CWA Gold Dagger and the Miles Franklin. Others seen at that podium on more than one occasion include Peter Corris, Marele Day, Garry Disher, Michael Robotham and Shane Maloney—all of whom have contributed to this collection of essays.

Maloney was a recipient of the Lifetime Achievement Award in 2009, and as part of his prize received a decent bottle of claret. He reported later that he'd momentarily left the bottle with his things after the ceremony and when he returned the bottle had been 'flogged'. As crime writing reveals, there are dangers lurking around every corner in this world we live in.

The Ned Kelly Awards have never been about prize money or expensive silverware. The prestige of joining the list of past winners is enough for any writer to covet a 'Ned'. Publishers such as Allen & Unwin and Text Publishing have always been generous supporters and, more recently, we have secured the support of the Copyright Agency.

Since those first years, the format of the award evenings has changed little. When Rosemary Cameron became director of the Melbourne Writers Festival, we moved from the fringe to become part of the main program of the festival and gained a new lease of life.

We have used different venues, but the formula hasn't changed. A host for the evening usually sets the tone and the debate features various authors and prominent figures in the crime community such as lawyers, judges and journalists.

By 2006 the Ned Kelly Awards had notched up just over a decade. The MWF program decided to do something special to mark the occasion. Thus the state attorney-general, Rob Hulls, was invited to present an opening address. Like everything else associated with the Neds, the brief was clear-cut: Crime.

The machinations of delivering a politician to a public event, even one as unassuming as the Ned Kelly Awards, were complex. The topic had to be more specific, we were told, so that parliamentary staff could ensure the speech was correctly 'fashioned'. Similarly, start times and finish times had to be stipulated. Who would meet the attorney-general? Where would they greet him? All of these things were perversely alien to the way the 'Neds' normally operated, but I attempted to satisfy the minister's office in a series of emails and phone calls. Also perversely, if not by design, the debate topic set for that night was 'that Australian crime writing is only concerned with the entertainment factor, not the big issues'. On the bill were Rhys Muldoon, Leigh Redhead, Greg Fleet and Tara Moss.

The house was packed by the time Rob Hulls was ushered onto the tiny stage. His minder had made it known on the short walk from car to venue that Mr Hulls was on a tight schedule. Hulls took to the stage with expected ease to promptly announce he had put together a speech that he hoped would reflect the spirit of the event.

Having done the honours by congratulating the Neds on reaching this milestone, Hulls proceeded to deliver a speech on the subject of crime that floored everyone present and had the audience laughing throughout and cheering at the end. He was ushered away by his minders and host Jane Clifton announced the teams for the debate.

There have been a number of memorable debates over the years and numerous authors and associated professionals have participated with relish. This one was particularly memorable as panellists warmed to the subject—'Crime is better than sex'—in front of a full house at the 'Festival Club' in Federation Square.

Jane Clifton, a wonderful host who ensures the pace never falters, was sitting at the edge of the stage, watching things unfold. The first and second speakers had finished. The final speaker for the affirmative took her place at the podium. Halfway through her presentation, she signalled the sound technician and loud burlesque music filled the room.

The volume increased and the audience looked to the stage for some understanding. By now the third speaker, crime novelist Leigh Redhead, was moving to the music, stepping into the spotlight and beginning the unmistakable gyrations of a striptease, as various items of clothing were removed. The Ned Kelly Awards have been witness to a range of unusual and colourful situations over the years, but Leigh Redhead's underwear set another benchmark.

The awards have always been about entertainment as well as celebrating talent, which is why they have come to represent the benchmark in Australian crime writing and revealed the vast pool of talent at work in this country.

Our local crime writers are now sought by overseas publishers and translated into dozens of languages and short-listed for international awards. Some years ago

Michael Robotham noted that winning the Ned Kelly had triggered a flood of emails and congratulatory bottles of champagne from his international publishers. When he asked them why it mattered, he was told that from then on he would always be marketed as 'an award-winning' writer. Other authors have told me similar stories of how important and coveted these odd-shaped gongs have become. The award winners are announced on major crime websites, blogs and in mystery magazines around the world.

This is gratifying for the many people who conceived, organised and worked towards the ongoing success of the Ned Kelly Awards. To this end the publication of *If I Tell You, I Will Have to Kill You*, with contributions so generously provided by so many talented Australian authors, will be a major step to ensuring Ned Kelly marches on into the future of Australian crime writing.

Peter Lawrance is the long-time convener and organiser of the Ned Kelly Awards, who has been instrumental in keeping the awards going and promoting the genre in Australia. Peter is currently working on his own crime novel.

AUTHORS' MUST-READS

Dickens, Charles *Bleak House*

Disher, Garry *Wyatt*

Dostoevsky, Fyodor *Crime and Punishment*

Durrell, Lawrence *The Alexandria Quartet*

Early English elegies

Fitzgerald, F. Scott *The Great Gatsby*

Flaubert, Gustave *Madame Bovary*

Fleming, Ian *From Russia with Love*

Giarratano, Leah *Vodka Doesn't Freeze*

Graves, Robert *The Reader Over Your Shoulder*

The Greek myths

Grenville, Kate *Dark Places*

Hall, Steven *The Raw Shark Texts*

Halligan, Marion *Valley of Grace*

Hardy, Thomas *The Mayor of Casterbridge*

Hemingway, Ernest *A Moveable Feast*

—— *For Whom the Bell Tolls*

Hendricks, Vickie *Miami Purity*

Herr, Michael *Dispatches*

Hiaasen, Carl *Skintight*

Higgins, George V. *The Friends of Eddie Coyle*

Hill, Reginald *On Beulah Height*

Høeg, Peter *Miss Smilla's Feeling for Snow*

Hooper, Chloe *The Tall Man: Death and Life on Palm Island*

Hopkins, Gerard *Manley The Lantern out of Doors*

Hughart, Barry *Bridge of Birds*

Hughes, Robert *The Fatal Shore*

Hyland, M.J. *This is How*

Irving, John *A Prayer for Owen Meany*

Johns, Captain W.E. *Biggles Flies South*

King, Stephen *On Writing*

Laden, Nina *Private I. Guana: The Case of the Missing Chameleon*

le Carré, John *Call for the Dead*

—— *The Spy Who Came in from the Cold*

Leonard, Elmore *Get Shorty*

—— *LaBrava*

Lewis, Ted *Jack's Return Home*

McCarthy, Cormac *The Road*

McDermid, Val *The Wire in the Blood*

McEwan, Ian *Atonement*

McGeachin, Geoffrey—any title

Mainwaring, Marion *Murder in Pastiche*

Maugham, W. Somerset *The Complete Short Stories (3 vols)*

Mosley, Walter *Devil in a Blue Dress*

Nin, Anaïs *The Diaries of Anaïs Nin*

O'Connell, Carol *The Judas Child*

Ondaatje, Michael *The English Patient*

Orwell, George *The Collected Essays, Journalism and Letters (4 vols)*

Paton, Alan *Cry, the Beloved Country*

Pearson, Ridley *The Pied Piper*

Poetry—good poetry from any epoch

Porter, Liz *Written on the Skin*
Robinson, Marilynne *Gilead*
Rowley, Hazel *Tete-a-tete: Simone de Beauvoir and Jean-Paul Sartre*
Roy, Arundhati *The God of Small Things*
Russell, Bertrand *Why I am Not a Christian*
Sacks, Oliver *The Man who Mistook his Wife for a Hat*
Salinger, J.D. *For Esme—With Love and Squalor*
Sayers, Dorothy L. *The Nine Tailors*
Schwarz-Bart, André *The Last of the Just*
Shakespeare—complete works
Shan, Han *(Cold Mountain) The Collected Songs of Cold Mountain*
Simenon, Georges *Inspector Maigret and the Killers* (or one of his many others)
Simon, David *Homicide: A Year on the Killing Streets*
Simon, Robert I. *Bad Men do what Good Men Dream: A Forensic Psychiatrist Illuminates the Darker Side of Human Behavior*
Sjöwall, Maj and Wahlöö, Per—entire series of the Inspector Beck novels
Stoker, Bram *Dracula*
Süskind, Patrick *Perfume*
Swarup, Vikas *Q & A*
Tartt, Donna *The Little Friend*
—— *The Secret History*
Temple, Peter *The Broken Shore*

Thompson, Jim *Pop. 1280*
Thompson, Hunter S. *Fear and Loathing in Las Vegas*
Thompson, Peg & Usukawa, Saeko (editors) *The Little Black and White Book of Film Noir*
Tolkien, J.R.R. *The Lord of the Rings*
Welsh, Louise *The Cutting Room*
Willeford, Charles *Miami Blues*